14.95   DOUBLE SIGNED

Naomi Hansen   (only

2007   Amazon

Biography of Elder and

Sister Farmer's son

D1569672

TIM FARMER

...A KENTUCKY WOODSMAN RESTORED

by

Steve Flairty

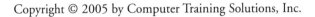

International Standard Book Number 0-9772280-0-2
Library of Congress Card Catalog Number 2005932119

Cover design and book layout by Asher Graphics
Cover photo by Scott Hayes

Manufactured in the United States of America

All book order correspondence and speaking engagement inquiries should
be addressed to:

CTS, Inc.
401 Lewis Hargett Circle
Lexington, KY 40503

800-262-1771

flairty@kentuckymonthly.com

www.timfarmeroutdoors.com

Dedication

To Edward Pribble, my great-grandfather and father of Grandma Flairty.   He was a true Kentucky gentleman and a superb story-teller.

Table of Contents

Acknowledgements

I've discovered that writing a biography requires the cooperation of not only the subject of the biography, but of a whole host of others who can relate stories, share insights, help the author develop a workable chronology of life events and add color to formerly sketchy remembrances. As I've mentioned to many in the writing of this book, Tim Farmer's bio is based on my experiences with him, studying dozens of his *Kentucky Afield* segments and talking to scores of his family, friends and acquaintances. All told, hundreds of hours have been invested in taking a peek at who, I'm convinced, is a truly inspirational individual. It has, for sure, been up close and personal communication, from being "in the woods or on the water" with him, to worshipping in a small church in Denton, Kentucky with his parents, Jerry and Sherry Farmer—two wonderful, caring people who were always there to help, but trusted me, as author, to make the big decisions about what to write.

To those people who know Tim and offered their words, *thank you. You were essential.* This was not a book that could be written while hiding away in the library next to the reference section.

For guiding me through the steps in structuring the book, I'm indebted to Mike Embry, my editor at *Kentucky Monthly.* Thanks for long ago showing confidence in a school teacher who simply "writes a little on the side."

Thanks to David and Lalie Dick for showing me the value of a tape recorder and the importance of developing a nose for stories, Jerrie Oughton for giving me more credit than I deserve and David Faust, who published my first magazine piece in *The Lookout.*

To all my former students at the School for the Creative and Performing Arts, here is the book I promised you when I left. Thanks for loving me!

And, of course, thank you, Tim! When I had my most perplexing moments, I always considered what a certain one-armed man's attitude might be. Then I proceeded to figure out a way to make it work.

Steve Flairty

Foreword

Whether in his buckskin jacket or khaki safari shirt, Tim Farmer carries a genuine air about him of pure Kentucky woodlore. He breathes it, he eats it, he lives it. As a personal friend, I can attest his character to be a little bit Daniel Boone, with a hint of Elvis rolled in.

My acquaintance with Tim Farmer started in 1998 at a sports show in Louisville, Kentucky. I was the local "bowfishing guru," and Tim wanted to do a segment on bowfishing for *Kentucky Afield*, an outdoor television show which he hosts. I knew of his show, and I knew of his disability, or as Tim says, his "physical aggravation," but I didn't really know that much more about him. I agreed to take him and his camera crew out on the lake.

Tim was shooting a compound bow at the time, holding it with his only good arm, the left arm, and drawing the string by clamping his teeth into a piece of nylon webstrap attached to the bowstring. Drawing the bow back with his neck muscles, he would take aim and release the arrow by relaxing the webstrap between his jaw teeth. Needless to say, I was impressed. Especially when he stacked three arrows into the bulls-eye, all of them touching one another. After demonstrating his shooting technique, and with a boyish grin, he handed me his bow and asked me to draw it. Surely this skinny guy who shot with his teeth must have a light draw. My face turned a bit red when I grunted and squirmed to yank back the 70 lb. pull bow that he shot so gracefully. I told him if he wanted to shoot fish that he'd have to leave that 70 pounder at home. I agreed to set up a recurve bow for him the night before we were to meet at the lake. Setting up a 53 lb. recurve with his mouth tab, I thought I'd shoot a couple of arrows the "Tim" way. It couldn't be that hard. Clamping down with my jaw teeth, I pushed the riser forward, drawing the string about three inches back, when an extreme pain shot through my neck and jaw. This is one capable dude, I thought.

The trip to the lake was a success. With the camera rolling, Tim easily hit just about every fish he shot at, matching me shot for shot, which humbled me just a bit more. I had been bowfishing for 20 years, while he had been doing it for 20 minutes. Yep, one capable dude.

How capable? Well, let's put it this way. He can out-shoot and outhunt the average hunter, and that's ditto for fishing, though he's a bit slow on baiting a hook. As our friendship grew, so did my admiration for his determined spirit to succeed. I've traveled from Michigan to Florida with him, covering a variety of outdoor adventure. I've witnessed him taking doubles in the dove field, swinging his shotgun on target with the finesse that a two-armed man would envy. The same goes for his ability with a fly rod. It really shouldn't work for him, but it does. We've fished for sharks with heavy tackle in the Florida Keys with Tim strapping on a PVC pipe device around his hips to hold a heavy saltwater rod. Let's just say it looked a bit…ah…odd. Tim playfully shrugged and summed it up with his typical "A man's got to do what a man's got to do."

His ability to handle his physical challenges is so normal for him that many times I actually forget that he is basically a one-armed guy. The simplest things we take for granted everyday, he takes as a mission to get accomplished, yet you will never hear him whine. It's no wonder he chose the Marine

Corps when he joined the service. One weekend, we bowhunt-
ed northeastern Kentucky using a friend's cabin. We got up
before first light and loaded up our gear, consisting of bows,
fanny packs and treestands. Swinging his treestand up on his
left shoulder, he grabbed the rest of his gear in his left hand, and
we walked the quarter mile from the truck to our morning spot.
I was running the camera that morning, and he instructed me
to get up my tree first so he could secure and steady the expen-
sive piece of video equipment I was to haul up, via a rope, to
me. After I secured the camera, he attached his climbing treestand to his tree. For those not familiar, a "climber" consists of
a platform for your feet and a hand climber to hang on to as
you lift your platform up with your legs, enabling you to climb
the tree in an inchworm-like manner. Some would've said it
looked painful, and let there be no doubt that it was. Tim lives
with pain every day of his life. But, I marveled as Tim used the
hand-climber with his one arm to climb that tree, six inches at
a time, until he was 20 feet up. I kept the camera rolling the
entire time, hoping that one day the piece may be archived so
others less fortunate may see that, indeed, if there is a will, there
is a way...Tim's way.

Tim's sense of humor is truly a gift. His ability to laugh
at what life hurls at him makes him the character he is. During
another hunt, we were taking a siesta break in a friend's house
when I thought I'd check on my buddy. Walking into the den,
I witnessed quite a sight that didn't really soak in for a while.
Tim had his left hand on the coffee table *and* his right foot---
his bare right foot. Between his hand and foot was a nail clip-
per, which he worked with his big toe to clip his fingernails.
"Now, *that's* impressive," I told my friend.

"Yeah, but I'm not worth a darn at hanging wallpaper,"
he laughed back at me. Yep, a man's got to do what a man's got
to do...and Tim Farmer does it so well.

I surmise that Tim's ability to succeed in all aspects of
the great outdoors has much to do with his passion to listen and

learn. His ability to converse with paupers or kings makes him the likeable person he is. I have observed old-timers bending Tim's ear on how to do this or that, what to look for, the how, when, and whys. At first, I thought he was only being polite by remaining quiet, nodding his head, with his occasional, "Is that right?" But I soon realized that he was recording everything said, adding to his plethora of woodlore knowledge. Comments made to me over the years, like, "What a good guy," only come because the enthusiasm in his eyes is genuine when you talk to him. Tim Farmer has never met a stranger.

This book, which is long overdue, tells of a man who looks frustration in the eye everyday…and spits.

May we be inspired to think a bit more like Tim Farmer, on those days we think we *"can't."*

Walt Kloeppel

The Woodsman

At home among lofty ridges and deep hollows, he interprets
The language of the creatures seeking refuge beneath towering trees.
There, beyond building and boulevard, he sits---with back against
The smooth, gray bole of a beech tree. Rooted thoughts search
The dark, rich soil where fern and fungi flourish.

The spider, master of design, spins silken stays to span the range
Between two branches of a dogwood. Ants scramble in unpredictable
Patterns across the floor of leaf mold. Two crows on the wing assault
The silence with raucous calls. A deer, from guarded stance, steps
Out of the tangled thicket onto a winding track rutted by hoof and claw.
Wisdom resounds in the soft cooing of a dove. Stringent time slowly dissolves-
Lost in the verdant spirit of the woodland. Peace is its own reward.

Restored, he returns with a rush, our wood-wise son. With him comes
The vital fragrance of earth, wind, and sun. His words are akin
To the waters of a wooded stream---rippled waves of sound woven
With song; threaded with strands of sunlight.

Sherry A. Farmer

Introduction

The first time I heard Tim Farmer's name was through a mutual friend. I was attending the Kentucky Book Fair in Frankfort and ran into Roger Singleton, the parent of a former student in my fourth grade class at a Lexington public school. Telling Roger of my new career as a senior correspondent for *Kentucky Monthly* magazine, he immediately suggested a story for me.

"I've got a guy somebody needs to do a story on," said Roger. "He lost the use of his right arm in a motorcycle accident about 20 years ago, but he can do about anything anyone else can do. He's real dynamic, one of the most upbeat people I've ever met, a real inspiration."

Trying to be polite, I asked Roger this person's name and what he did for a living. Frankly, lots of people have asked me about doing an article on a person, place or idea.

"His name's Tim Farmer and he is the host of that outdoors program on public TV," Roger said.

Not a serious hunter or fisherman myself, I wasn't immediately attracted to the idea, but as Roger and I made the rounds at the book fair, he kept talking about Tim Farmer.

"He goes out to places like Shriners, Cardinal Hill and schools to talk and he's always a big hit. I go with him sometimes and it seems like everyone knows him and wants to talk to him," Roger continued.

Then, Roger mentioned something that perked up my ears. Something most unusual. "Tim shoots a bow and arrow by pulling the arrow back with his teeth! Not only that, he uses his mouth to crank the reel when he fishes and he shoots a rifle, accurately, with one arm."

When Roger said that, I figured that a person with that kind of determination had to be something special, almost bigger than life. Can you imagine the raw discipline involved? I pitched the idea to my editor and publisher, and although the magazine doesn't normally do a lot of fishing and hunting articles, they saw something special, too, and they gave me the go-ahead to do the story. It later appeared as a cover article and received a lot of positive response.

In the process of doing research for the article, I casually mentioned that the Tim Farmer story might be the subject for a book because of its inspirational value. It seemed to me like there was something more than a straight fishing and hunting story. Roger, of course, agreed, though I was not quite ready for the commitment to be the author. Tim was certainly flattered but thought himself undeserving of the attention. Besides, he was just doing what came "unnatural." About a year later, I decided I could give the book thing a try. Approached again, Tim had softened. He considered the fact that people contact him regularly, asking for advice in managing their own disabilities or just seeking an encouraging word. He helped many, particularly those hoping to learn bow shooting with the mouth. He has tried to be available and listen to the individuals he meets daily, giving them a simple message---get active, don't feel sorry for yourself and find a way to do the things you love. Realizing that he's been given a platform to speak to others, he agreed to do the book. Tim now feels he can reach a much larger audience.

The book relates events that have shaped Tim's life early on and reflects about people who have profoundly influenced him. It chronicles his struggles to restore the happy life of his childhood to one just as satisfying in adulthood. Along the way, we'll see how Tim Farmer has touched others. My hope is that you'll see Tim the person, one who thrives on passion followed by action, one who believes life daily has something great in store for those who seek it with determination. And, I hope you'll see one who believes in unselfishly giving back to the world–a world he calls his playground.

In her poem, *The Woodsman*, Tim's mother Sherry uses both the literal woodland, her son's most precious source of life energy, and the magic of metaphor to produce a picture of an individual who once lost a vital limb, but not his own vitality. He is one, she intimates, that by being in close touch with his beloved outdoors, has become *restored*…and having been restored, *he returns with a rush*, hoping to share his good news to many who are looking for a reason to hope and have a more satisfying life, regardless of challenging circumstances.

Tim is a whirlwind. Most people, at the end of their workday, are glad to go home, relax, turn the engine off. Not Tim. At Tim's invitation, I met him one hot day at the Game Farm, in Frankfort, after he had spent a day in fishing and hunting related work activities. What did Tim want to do? His boat was hitched to his pickup, ready for an evening trip to the Kentucky River. Did Tim want to lay back and take it easy on the "lazy river"? He probably deserved the treat, but did he? Well, you can put it this way. Four hours later we got back to shore. We had traveled 20 miles upstream, often racing at speeds of nearly 50 mph–the motorboat navigated gracefully by a one-armed man with a shock of wavy brown hair flopping in the wind. All along the route, we stopped along the shoreline and Tim furiously shot gar and buffalo carp with a bow and arrow. It had been a long day, but he was already planning a *Kentucky Afield* fishing segment to be filmed in Cumberland County next morning. The crew would meet at the studio at 6 a.m.and be on the water in a few hours.

Tim's been going like that since he was a happy kid in rural Kentucky. After a rough bump on his joyful road, the result of which still causes him daily "aggravations," he came back strong...and *restored*.

In reading the Tim Farmer story, you maybe should fasten your seat belt real tight. The guy moves pretty fast, does a lot, lives a lot of life. Get some rest before hand. He may wear you out just reading about him.

1

Accident

The slender, brown-haired 20-year-old glanced back at his parents, waving heartily as he nosed his Kawasaki KZ40 onto Highway 7. The roar of the engine and the cool feel of the wind emblazoned him with a sense of power. He wore an approved, official looking motorcycle helmet, but the T-shirt he wrapped over his wiry upper body was cut across, halfway down, a product of 1984 youth culture. It was five miles to Grayson, Kentucky, where he would merge onto I-64 and enjoy sunny, cloudless weather on his trip to Louisville. There, he would meet up with two other Marine buddies and ride with them in a car to Millington Naval Air Base near Memphis, a six-hour drive.

Life was splendid for Tim Farmer on this beautiful Sunday afternoon in June. Already a person wired with infectious optimism, Tim had a lot of reasons to feel upbeat. He had successfully completed the grueling, 13-week Marine boot camp, an important start to what could well be a career in military service–long dreamed about. In the Corps, he even met a few guitar pickers who shared his love of music and wanted to collaborate in a recording studio. Breezing along on the tree-lined road and smelling the freshly cut hay fields, he thought about the fun he had fishing this weekend, the game in the woods he would always have to hunt, his fiancé he had just spent time with and their plan to someday raise a family together. He grinned when he thought about his friend, Phillip, a fellow woodsman and partner in many small-town adventures and pranks, little items that just drove his mother, Sherry, crazy. It was so comforting to know she loved her Timmy anyway.

He had just checked his few saddle bags, making sure everything he carried was travel-tight. He wanted no distractions after he left Grayson. Wheeling onto the merging ramp at a moderate speed, Tim noticed the pavement was dusty, covered with an unusual amount of loose gravel and sand. Experience had shown him this signaled a possible problem for a motorcycle. A planner by nature and still in control, thoughts flowed through his mind about how he would land if he lost his balance and took an unceremonial spill. In an instant, a hard rubbing noise overpowered all other sounds. His meager plans, he discovered, were of no help. He felt his heart drop out of his chest as he lost road traction. During those fleeting moments, any sense of control deserted him. He saw, and felt, a slow motion, ugly blur hanging like a cloud around his wide open eyes. Then the hard stuff came. He felt his body and machine together jerk like a whiplash against the hard, gray railing. The impact was cruel, heartless and immediate—an ambush. No more thinking, no more preparing. It was happening now. Tim was experiencing a motorcycle wreck, pure and simple. It was not a minor one, either...

Near the bottom of the bank, Tim shakily stood up, then managed a foggy look at his battered motorcycle. A quick, sentimental thought, back to the day he bought the bike against his parents' wishes, surfaced. There was no time for old memories now, however. He felt beat up and knew he would need some help, and real soon. He reached for his now bothersome helmet, grasped it and pulled. For reasons unknown, it wouldn't break loose. Then, inexplicably, he heard what sounded like water pouring out of a huge pitcher, and it hit the ground with a torrential force. He quickly recognized it as blood, lots of it. Instinctively, the Marine training maxim regarding battlefield wounds flashed into his mind. *Stop the blood, stop the blood. Stay alert, stay alert.* He lurched at the right bicep area with his left hand, slowing down the flow of the warm, red life source. Reading the situation realistically, he knew he was going to need help, and very soon.

Somehow, his young, muscular body leaned forward and ambulated upwards to the dented guardrail. He stepped guardedly over the rail and stood next to the ramp, thoroughly weakened, dazed and intermittently confused. A dull awareness of discomfort in his right hip was bothersome, and Tim cringed as he noticed a widened gap of open tissue between the two outer fingers on his left hand. No pleasure, but there was not, as yet, any significant pain. What seemed to be nearly a dozen cars drove by him, slowing and gawking—but none stopped to offer assistance. Just when a wave of fresh frustration flowed through his now delicate psyche, he felt himself losing physical strength. Then, momentarily, he lay directly in the middle of the ramp, face up.

He lay still, so still he could sense the turning of the earth on its axis, like he was moving slowly, so slowly, on a carnival ride with approving loved ones all about him. Paradoxically, considering the circumstances, Tim was taken in by the irradiating sun, the air's warmth, the softness of the white clouds. A feeling of quiet, sweet peace rested inside him for an indefinite time. It was an odd sensation. He knew he didn't really want to die, but if he must, he was ready…

After what seemed like hours, but probably only a few short minutes, Tim could make out the shadowy outline of a police officer standing over him. The euphoric feeling of peace had slipped away, replaced by a hard realism, even sadness. Tim realized where the main source of the cascading blood had originated. It was his right bicep and shoulder area—and it was one gory mess. Not only could he see the macabre, ripped hunk of sinewy tissue, but hard, throbbing pain was rudely making its uninvited presence known. Now, being in the moment, Tim was aware of a horrible, sudden change from what a short while ago was youthful, optimistic bliss.

The policeman's face and demeanor told Tim that this was a very, very ugly scene.

"Can't you just go ahead and put me down…now?" Tim managed with a voice as strong as he could muster, his trademark sense of humor intact.

The officer's countenance drew even more morbid, then apologetic.

"Well, legally I can't do—."

"I know that…just joking, officer," Tim said. "Don't you know I was just joking?"

The officer was bewildered by the victim's condition— and his personal disposition at a time such as this. It wasn't normal to watch a dying person joke. Cursing, maybe.

Tim felt himself weakening further. Frustrated, he fought like a good Marine to keep his consciousness, as if it was his solemn birthright. And now, vaguely coming from some place far in the distance, he could hear could hear the wailing sound of a siren. And, yes, he knew it was coming for Tim Farmer, formerly a recruit, now a U.S. Marine…and maybe, soon, not either. *This is getting to be pretty serious stuff, he thought.* Strangely, he was not overly nervous.

More moments passed, then Tim could sense the cautious care the EMT's were taking with his body as his dead weight was lifted onto the stretcher. He felt helpless and totally dependent as two men maneuvered him into the ambulance. Settled in the cubicle, Tim visually examined his new surroundings. A twinge of anger hit him. Expecting so much more than he saw, he found himself in a bland, sterile environment that didn't even look medical. Further disconcerting, a towel lay over much of his injured limb, but enough showed to reveal an odd, washed out whiteness in the arm. His class ring, still on his right hand, became a sort of beacon to his now former life. Glancing back to the "good" left limb, Tim noticed a finger pointed away from the others, probably broken.

The experience was surreal, dream-like, foggy. He wondered how things could change so fast. He floated in and out of consciousness, and he wondered if anybody had a plan to help him. The attendant gazed out the back window, looking for all the world to not be interested in the present patient. Frightfully, Tim could discern no evidence of the EMT being trained to respond to a patient in trauma. That was immediately clear.

"Do you think I'm going to make it?" Tim managed.

"I dunno."

"Shouldn't you try to talk to me?"

The attendant continued to look away, saying something unintelligible. He was clearly incompetent.

With all his weakened might, Tim came on direct, even stern to the attendant. *"You need to come over here and talk to me."*

No response.

Tim reasoned that he might as well have been lying there all by himself. His thoughts were racing. *Where did they get this guy, off a garbage truck? Shouldn't somebody be trying to keep me conscious?...Don't let me lose it... Somebody talk to me, let me know what is going on...*

The ambulance sped on.

Tim now would take a different Sunday afternoon drive, not by his choice. The siren, the urgent speed of the ambulance and his own instincts painted an ominous picture, and it was nearly overwhelming. He was unsure of the destination of the emergency vehicle, and at this point, he didn't know if he really cared. He simply tried to stay awake.

2

Hospitals

Tim awakened, relieved that he was alive. He was in a Cabell Huntington Hospital bed, about 40 miles from Grayson and in West Virginia. Firmly in place was a tube in his nose and throat. His right hand—black and blue and outrageously bloated—hung above and in front of him like an undesirable character taunting him. His right pelvic bone area, fractured, reminded him that he was hurt in more places than his upper extremities. Even his smallest movements, he noticed right away, were snail-like and mostly painful. He'd have to decide if the efforts were worth it. Tim was heavily and uncomfortably medicated and he struggled with a hazy perception of his new environment.

Time was hard to fathom, but pretty soon he saw, and heard, people he recognized only vaguely. They moved near the bedside. It was like a steady parade of friendly, dream-like ghosts hovering over and keeping a watchful eye on their good friend. Friendly or not, Tim didn't want to be there in that bed, at that time, in that hospital.

Always there were his parents. Sherry mostly stayed with Tim during the day while Jerry was there at night after work. Sherry was particularly worried about the chances of Tim getting out of bed and, because of being heavily medicated, falling. His sister Deborah stayed at his bedside as much as possible.

And though Tim didn't want to be at the hospital, he "never complained," Deborah said. "As kids growing up, we were always fussing with each other. We were so different, but then we'd always take up for each other, too. As it turned out, he was always calling for me while he was in the hospital bed and going through all his pain."

One of his visitors was a good buddy, Larry Thompson, who appeared with a look on his face not unlike the police officer at the accident scene. Larry had been a newcomer to Grayson back in Tim's high school days. He was a person Tim had taken it on himself to befriend. Larry was considered somewhat different, and many of his new classmates shunned him. As Larry respectfully moved closer to his ailing friend, he clumsily and inadvertently struck the bed, an action that unleashed all the demons of hell to inflict pain on the vulnerable body of one Tim Farmer.

Tim's primal scream of anguish was heard by what seemed to be everybody in the hospital. Larry felt horrible about his mistake, but Tim didn't hold on to his anger any longer than the pain lasted. It's a bolt of lightning he'll never forget, though. When circumstances allowed later, Tim made a deliberate effort to visit Larry's step-father, also a patient in the hospital with a serious illness. Tim and Larry are good friends today.

For weeks, however, the agonizing pain of nurses dressing his right arm wounds rivaled the pain that Larry caused with his simple blunder.

"The nurses were really very nice to me and they knew how bad it hurt. They would often try to soothe me by rubbing my hair when they were working with the bandages," Tim said recently.

Cabell Huntington Hospital reported to Sherry and Jerry that Tim was doing well–"except for his right arm."

"I didn't keep a log of what happened during that time, but it was all so very hard on us," Sherry said.

"Unlike Tim, Sherry and I were totally devastated," Jerry said. "We didn't know what to think, especially the way Tim was so active and everything."

Tim was cognizant of his parents' deep concern.

"It was such a monumental burden on them. Dad would try to joke. Mom tried to joke, too, but I'd see her face twitching a lot. Mom would help me bathe and shave. But they often didn't know what to do or how to react," he said recently. "I remember Mom saying things to me about the beauty of the Colorado mountains, trying everything she could just to make me feel better."

"Tim wasn't cracking jokes, but he was prepared to have them do whatever needed to be done," said Sherry.

Tim found out from a nurse, bluntly, that he would no longer have the use of his right arm.

"At the time, I thought the nurse was pretty rough in telling me. I actually argued with him about it. I mean, how could that guy know that for sure? I got real mad. But once I found that out for sure, I dealt with it. I guess the guy thought he was helping me. I had one bad night, but I never really got depressed through the whole thing."

Tim received surgery on his right arm at Cabell. Irrevocable nerve damage was the sad and true story. No miracles were performed. Tim couldn't use his right arm when he entered the hospital—nor when he left.

"All it did was patch things up some on the arm. The srugery didn't do much to help me," he said. "The arm was still a real big mess."

Realizing that he would likely face a lifetime of left-handedness, he began to practice writing with that hand.

"I had been *very* right-handed," he said, "and so my early writing as a left-hander was just really horrible."

Another way he practiced his dexterity was to work on an airplane model his father had brought to the hospital. As he developed dexterity, he also grew, inch by inch, in badly needed patience and mental discipline. It was an attribute that Tim formerly had reserved for hunting, fishing and music.

Tim was going to need some serious care for a long time, and he soon was transferred to Bethesda Hospital in Maryland, a military hospital. "I vaguely remember being transported in an ambulance to a plane. When I got to Bethesda, I was essentially stuck in a kind of 'holding room,' where I just waited, waited...," he said. "I was in a room with a Navy guy who stuttered very badly. There were so many around me who had so many kinds of injuries. There were guys who had motorcycle accidents, horse-back riding accidents. One person I met was a wild kind of guy who drank rubbing alcohol. I even saw people there who were eating plastic flowers."

The first few months in the hospital were spent "in a fog," said Tim, "mostly brought on by taking all kinds of pain medication. I watched a lot of TV and slept a lot. I got my days and nights all turned around. I watched movies late into the night and I'd wake up, half-way through them. The pain would get so bad I could hardly stand it. I'd ring a little bell, they'd come and give you a shot and you'd be out. It was that way over and over again. You just sat there and waited all the time."

He waited around so much that he finally had to get up and out of the bed. Getting out of bed was good for him in two ways. For the born hyperactive Tim, it got him moving. It also served as a distraction, a way of keeping his mind preoccupied and off the unforgiving pain. He uses his passions and his hobbies that way today, taking few, if any, medications.

"Even then, when I felt so bad, I looked for adventure.

I was able to find the way to climb up on top of the Bethesda roof. It was real high and I had a great view of Washington, and I would spend hours there."

After his stint at Bethesda, Tim was sent to Walter Reed Hospital in Washington, D.C. There, another surgery was performed, one that would transplant nerves from his legs to his right arm. Tim thought it was an unnecessary operation. "They had let me see the report before hand, and it said that it probably wouldn't work. But for some reason they did it anyway," he said.

As predicted, the surgery did little to help Tim's right arm. The procedure put metal staples in his legs, though, and in only a few days he was told, sternly and repeatedly by a doctor, to "get up and walk." In other words, it was time for a little physical therapy.

Uncharacteristically, Tim became livid toward the doctor and refused to comply. "The skin was cracking open in my legs and I couldn't even let my legs hang off the side of the bed because it hurt so bad. It was too soon to be doing that kind of thing. I just told them I was going back to bed."

If that wasn't hard enough, a tube placed in his arm for the surgery was removed, or perhaps more accurately, "jerked out."

"It could have been that they were mad at me for not doing the physical therapy, but probably not. When they ripped it out, it was like I got hit hard by lightening and I went out completely. Then they kept telling me every day to 'get up and walk,' get up and walk.'"

The endless hours he spent at Walter Reed brought on more fits of stir-crazy boredom and a hankering for changing his routine. When Tim was able to start walking again, he maneuvered his way out of the hospital for walks that would take him to the D.C. subways, then to the Smithsonian Museum, the Natural History Museum, all the monuments and even to the zoo.

"The hospital didn't care where you went," he said, "and when I went out, I found that people would look at you a little different (because of the right arm disability). I don't like to be stared at. I'd rather people come up and ask me directly about my arm than stare."

Tim was losing a lot of weight. Tired of the hospital food served him in his room, he once asked a nurse about what he could do to get better food. "She told me that the food was OK down in the cafeteria, that I just ought to get up and walk down there and get something good to eat," he said. "Being in a hospital can be humiliating anyway, but here I was, wearing a robe that pretty much left your backside exposed, a pair of pajama bottoms and these little blue shoes made of paper and elastic. So I shuffled on down, very conscious of the way I looked. I filled my tray with all kinds of good food and a drink. I took it to the cashier to pay. But then, I had the drink sitting too far to the left. It unbalanced the tray, and everything slid off onto the floor."

What happened next became a defining moment in the post-accident Tim Farmer.

"When I dropped everything on the floor, everyone just looked at me. The place got deathly quiet. No one even offered to help me. It was humiliating. I just sat the tray back down, wandered out of the cafeteria and back up to my hospital room."

His foundation was shaken. Something became clear, even compelling to Tim Farmer when the incident happened. "I knew then that everything was going to be different in my life, that I was going to have to understand that and make the best of it. Right there in that military hospital cafeteria, I had a realization that I was no longer a two-handed person," he said. "I was a one-armed guy."

At one point in his stay at Walter Reed, he met another patient who had an impact on his evolving, and maturing, thought process. "I met this guy from the Navy who wrecked his motorcycle and lost the use of an arm, just like me. Actually, it was somewhat worse because he also had no use of his shoulder," said Tim. "Whenever I got around the guy he had this certain look in his eyes that was kind of disturbing. He was bitter and his surly expression would just never change. He'd show me pictures of himself before his accident, looking all buff and proud. Then he'd say, 'Look at me. *Now* look at me.' I kept trying to talk to him, but he just wasn't handling things very well."

A while later, Tim received the sad, but true, news. The guy with the disturbing look in his eyes had killed himself. To this day, Tim is alert to others who might have that look of despondency.

Tim was allowed to come home to Grayson from Walter Reed Hospital for short periods of convalescence. During these times, he was able to nourish the relationship with his girlfriend Cheryl. In September of 1984, Tim and Cheryl were married in Grayson. In a relatively short time, since June, a lot had happened in hunter, fisherman, musician, Marine and new husband Tim Farmer's life.

He was just getting started in the restoration process.

3

Makeover

There was no big ceremony when Tim was finally released from Walter Reed Hospital in 1985. No "manual for life" was given, no on-going training or transition counseling. Nearly a grueling year had passed with Tim spending time at three separate medical facilities. There he had ingested medications that left him drowsy and lifeless, spent hours watching TV, ate tasteless food–plus, he had an arm that didn't work anymore. His weight had fallen from 165 pounds to about 120. It was not the kind of existence that a hyperactive person who lived for the great outdoors, music and unbounded activity could learn to love. But though Tim had many questions yet unanswered and no specific plans, he was ready to leave the God-forsakened hospital environment and implement his plan for a life makeover.

Certainly not all of Tim's year of medical imprisonment was used simply killing time or doing busy work. Continually, he thought about the things he loved to do before the accident, things like fly fishing for panfish and bass, hunting rabbits and squirrels, turkeys and quails. He thought about cutting firewood, interacting with his dog, and playing music to his hearts content. He knew what a full life, one like he had growing up, was, and he sorely wanted to experience it again.

As much as is possible, Tim had no illusions about the changes he'd have to make to continue his passions. Enough time had passed, enough experiences were garnered since the accident for him to understand that fact. Not only his passions, but also daily, menial activities would become more than automatic rituals. Buttoning shirts, changing clothes, brushing teeth, clipping fingernails–the list is a small sampler of things that Tim formerly did in seconds that now would take many minutes, possibly longer.

"The brain is set up to have you use both hands in most of your activities," Tim said matter-of-factly, "so you have to train it to allow you to do things with just one hand. There is usually a way. You just have to figure out what it is."

Realizing and understanding his limits, Tim set himself on a course to figure out a way of doing the things he had always done. It was not a question of what activities he would simply cut from his schedule, or concentrating on daily life routines. He thought big thoughts, had big dreams. He set his mind to questions like: *How* can I fly fish? *How* can I hunt and shoot at rabbits with a shotgun? *How* can I hunt deer with a bow and arrow? *How* will I play my music? *How* will I drive my vehicle? *How* will I live a normal, productive life–and more?

Because of his disability, the Marine Corps honorably discharged him, much to his chagrin. "I begged them to allow me to stay," he said. "I took my pleas as high in the ranks as I possibly could. And what really bothered me was the fact that I felt rejected by them."

This was a tough pill to swallow for Tim Farmer, one individual who hoped to be a career Marine. Of huge concern, too, was an over-riding question. *If the Marine Corps didn't want him, who did?* He wasn't used to that kind of rejection.

Disappointed by the discharge but resigned to ending the military chapter of his life, Tim and his wife located in Grayson to be with family who knew and supported him, familiar places and friends he had lived and had fun with during his teen years. Drawing a Daniel Boone comparison, he had plenty of woodlands in Carter and Greenup Counties, with plentiful game. He had streams that were ideal for panfish and he adored Greenbo and Grayson Lakes. He had country fresh air to breathe, plus he had been given small, temporary disability pay from the Marine Corps at the time of his release. He also had a wife, Cheryl, to support, and money was a big issue.

"Everything came down to the wire each check," said Tim, who drove a $400 Plymouth Scamp at that time. "Cheryl pretty much had to take care of me, so she couldn't work. We'd go to the store and get chipped beef, eggs and macaroni and cheese. We had lots of chipped beef on toast, plus egg sandwiches. We had to be conscious of every dime we spent. It wasn't easy."

Despite the stress, there were enough positives around Grayson that Tim was invigorated, though a long way from being as happy as he wanted to be. At least, he thought, he was out of the hospital and now more free to make his own choices.

"It just so happened that it was squirrel hunting season when I got out of the hospital," Tim remembered. "This was time to go figure things out by going out in the woods. I took my .22 out and said, 'Hey, I can rest this on a branch and do just like I did before.' Gradually, when you use just one arm it gets pretty strong. Before long, I was able to shoot flying quails with a shotgun using my one good arm."

Jonathan, the younger bother, helped Tim work at his shooting accuracy by throwing clay pigeons in the air. He also had a part in improving Tim's left arm strength.

"We'd go out and play tennis and he absolutely didn't want his young brother to beat him. He played with his left arm and it helped build it up. It much improved his game. We'd play for hours, red-faced and panting. The competition we had really helped."

Not all the experiences were positive around the Grayson area, however. Tim recalled a scary episode in this transition time. "It was one of my first fishing trips. I was fishing on a deck and my friend fished on a motorboat. By accident, I fell in the lake. I was wearing a jacket and boots and my arm was in a sling. I hadn't even thought about swimming at this point and was scared to death," he said. "I grabbed onto the boat, but it was hard to hold on. My friend had trouble starting the boat to drag me out of the deep water, but finally I talked him through it and I made it to shallow water and walked to shore."

In coming back to Grayson, another difficult thing for Tim was the looks he received while out in public, something he encountered earlier when he took short trips out of the military hospitals. He considered it rudeness.

"My hand had gotten smaller and smaller through atrophy. It looked much like that of Bob Dole. I went into a Chinese restaurant and all these people were looking at me. It was like a wasp stinging me. I walked out of the restaurant. I wasn't depressed, but I just didn't want to be looked at like that. I was young and highly concerned about my appearance. That matter was extremely important to me at that point in my life, though it doesn't bother me as badly today," he said.

Tim's passion for doing lots of outdoor activities did battle against the frustrations he encountered while attempting them. Things like putting fishing line through eyeholes, untangling line, and taking a fish off the hook. If Tim saw a nest of fish just waiting to get caught, it might take him 15-20 minutes to get mobilized. Another aggravation might be batting gnats away from his face while holding a hunting rifle.

"The word is 'frustrating,' " said Tim recently, "you're always having to ask the question 'How do you do it?' So for the disabled person, you are constantly frustrated. Not that you're to the point you don't enjoy life, but if you're a busy person and want to accomplish things, it's constantly frustrating."

In the early years of marriage, it put strains on the relationship. "I wasn't mad at Cheryl, but I was just frustrated at trying to do things. I don't think she completely understood that, just like anybody else wouldn't. It was a real trying time."

It was also tough when it came to playing music. Tim played the banjo, mandolin–and, most passionately, the guitar.

"The guitar *was* my instrument," said Tim. "I grew up playing the guitar, and it was a huge loss, even my most profound loss, not being able to play like I wanted to. Sister Deborah knew it was a tough pill for Tim to swallow. "He was an absolutely fantastic guitar player before the accident," she said, "and it was really hard for him to give that up."

You mean Tim Farmer has given up on something he loves?

"Well, I tried to rig up some stuff and I still play a little lead. It's not the same, though. Mom and Dad had a tape of me thumb picking a song. It was all I could do just to listen to it, though. Probably some day we'll go back and try to do more work on the guitar, though."

The way Tim communicated those words, it seemed like he's looking for a way to have a fighting chance of excelling, much like he has done with hunting and fishing. He hasn't found it yet with the idea of finessing real good music out of his guitar with one hand, but don't dismiss him and the challenge yet. He's found a way to do so many other things before.

Even with limitations, though, he was able to use a multi-track recorder and lay out voice harmonies, which he said, "was fun. I could almost put a whole band together." And even when Tim wasn't producing music, he was always listening to it. He still hopes to make music an even bigger part of his future.

The four years after leaving the hospital were spent as trial and error ones and the results were often mixed. Under the category of positive experiences, however, were the births of two children. Elizabeth, born October 19, 1986, and Rebekah, December 15, 1987, brought some more joy into the Farmers' life.

"Both kids were great," he said. "They weren't bad about waking us up in the middle of the night and screaming and hollering. I was still a kid myself and I wanted to have fun playing with them. It was a wonderful time."

Looking at Tim Farmer during that period in his life, you might call those years the beginning stages of the second half of his life. Tim does for sure.

"I see my life basically divided into the part before the accident and the part after," Tim said.

One thing is for sure. The learning curve in the second half has probably been much steeper. He lives in a world where the majority do things with two arms. Practically all things he does are, at least at first, unnatural.

"Looking at what has happened, though, I don't believe I would have done as much with my life if it had not been for the accident," he said.

It's time to take a look at what has happened with Tim farmer's life since the accident.

4

Vocation

It was now 1988, four years after the fateful Sunday afternoon in Grayson. Father Time had taught Tim Farmer some lessons, and with the support of his wife, his parents and his friends around Grayson, he was developing his own special brand of normalcy. He was doing a lot of things that 24-year-olds with two arms do, but the way he did them was unorthodox, a product of his natural creativity and pure willpower–and they worked pretty well.

But Tim also had a question that was beginning to nag him incessantly, one that wouldn't wiggle off the hook. What was he going to do, *really do*, for his life's work?

It wouldn't be getting up at four a.m. working for Pony Express Courier Service, a place where he was employed for about a year. The money was decent, but long-term interest wasn't there. He had tried a year of school at Ashland Community College. There he took courses in history (all A's in his favorite subject) and English, toying with the idea of being a high school teacher. He even had some interest in the field of anthropology. He thought about following his father's field–drafting. These were just ideas passing through a sometimes impulsive mind, though, and they didn't take root. Nothing, in the end, really zinged him hard enough to commit himself. Help in his search came from an unexpected source.

"At that time, my next door neighbor, Jeff Adams, worked for the Kentucky Fish and Wildlife Department. He told me all about the things he did there. I told him, hey, I'd really like to work for them. So he encouraged me to go take the test," Tim said.

The test for Tim was relatively easy. It dealt with identifying kinds of fish, hunting and fishing, and knowledge of boating–all were things already ingrained in him. He did well.

"There were two fisheries technician jobs open and I applied to get one. I wanted the job so bad. I remember going into the interview with a new leather glove on my right hand (wearing a glove on the disabled arm's hand is a practice he continues today because the hand, due to the lack of circulation, gets cold easily). I'm sure it looked to them like 'Dr. Strangeglove' or something," he laughed. "I could tell they were concerned about what I was able to do with one hand. They asked some very specific questions. I told them to ask Jeff, my neighbor. He saw the kinds of things I did all the time. They could tell I was excited and really wanted the job."

After fretting for two weeks, Tim got good news. His exuberance and good test scores landed him the job. He started his fish and wildlife career in 1989 and moved his family to Frankfort "with everything we owned. It was a joyous time," and he was truly beaming.

The job met all expectancies. "I was in 'high cotton.' I had a uniform and a name tag and everything," Tim said. "We trap-netted, we gill-netted and we went out electro-fishing (a process that temporarily stuns fish so that personnel can more closely study them)."

Ironically, electro-fishing with Tim became a challenge for his co-workers–but not because he had only one arm. The boat that was used was 16 feet with a deck on the front. Twelve-feet poles were attached to the nets and hand-held by the technicians in order to dip the stunned fish. It's not hard to predict what might have happened in the procedure.

"I got so excited when I saw the fish get stunned that I was accidentally cracking everybody in the head with my pole," he said. Tim thinks now that the electro-fishing experience showed the others that he was going to be able to handle most aspects of his job with vigor and effectiveness.

"Actually, there wasn't anything he couldn't do," said Tim Slone, who worked with Tim. "He could do what everybody else did, he just did it with one hand. He just found ways to get it done."

Tim Farmer, it appeared, had found his niche. The disappointment of his Marine Corps career derailment had faded with time and the coming of his new job. His gig as a fish and wildlife technician, which eventually spanned six years, was a happy marriage of interests and vocation for the always fun-loving, outdoors-driven Tim Farmer–now making a living doing what he might gladly do for free. He was accepted and well liked by his fellow workers. He was so giddy that he found it easy to deal with the question he was asked continually, "What happened to your arm?

"I really had fun with that," he said. "I went from alligator stories, to sharks, to helicopters. I would try to beef it up every time. The last big one I told was that it was a horrible line dancing accident. The poor guys around me (who knew) had to put their heads down to keep from laughing. The guys at Fish and Wildlife are the greatest bunch of guys I've ever been around in my life."

During the time as a technician, he noticed that many of his co-workers at the department were using a bow and arrow, either to hunt or target shoot. Impulsively, Tim decided to join in on the fun.

"I had used a bow and arrow as a kid, and now I was dying to use one, too," he said. "So I went out and bought one, even though I had no idea how to draw one or anything." Now he had something else to figure out.

He termed his early attempts at shooting, using both feet and pulling with his left hand, as "an ungainly way to shoot. I mean, you can't be up in a deer stand and raise your legs to shoot." Tim knew he had to try a different approach, even if it might be drastic in scope.

"I heard about this guy, Biff Williams, in Washington state who had put a piece of leather on his bow and pulled back with his teeth. I scurried around work to get the guys to make me up a special piece of leather on my string. I tried it with 38 lbs. and within an hour was doing real well."

With help from fellow fisheries technician and experienced bow shooter Billy Mitchell, Tim was on his way. He put in the necessary practice and was all ears when Mitchell talked.

"Tim had such a child's inquisitiveness about him in trying to figure out a way to effectively shoot the bow," said Mitchell. "He just always had a 'can do' attitude about it." Mitchell also built a special deer stand for Tim and mentioned something that might be surprising. "Tim wanted it to be 10-feet tall, but I thought that was too high. Tim wasn't a real tree squirrel. He was more like a ground squirrel. After he got used to it, though, he got over some of his fear of heights."

To this day, Tim thinks he is a tree squirrel. "I *never* have had a fear of heights," he said.

On Tim's progress chart since leaving hospital care, learning how to be an archer by using his mouth to pull the arrow back was a huge measuring mark. The strides he made, however, were not without pain. He threw his energy into perfecting his newfound craft with almost reckless abandon. He began a grueling regimen of shooting arrows 150-200 times per day with a pressure of 50 lbs., then eventually 70 lbs. The prac-

tice brought a sore and sometimes bloody mouth–and a hunger
for competition. Using the teaching he received from Billy
Mitchell, he spent a year hunting with the bow and gained lots
of confidence in his accuracy. He then decided he would try his
archery skills in direct competition against able-bodied target
shooters–all around the country. The results were good, and he
actually won many of the contests. The reaction to his success
was, at times, comical. "People started complaining to the
authorities," Tim laughed, "that I had an unfair advantage. I
believe those guys just didn't want to go home and tell their
wives they got beat by a one-armed man."

Benjy Kinman, now Kentucky Division of Fisheries
director, remembered the first time Tim killed a deer with a
bow on property close to his own in Franklin County.

"He went out and got it himself," said Kinman, "and
brought it to my house. I showed him how to dress it. He was
pretty happy about it."

"I didn't know if I'd get one or not," Tim said proudly,
"but I thought I'd try. It was an eight-pointer, 180 lbs., a nice
deer."

In time, Tim branched out to a mixture of hunting and
fishing, called bow fishing. Using a special bow with a reel
mount, he was both able to shoot retrievable arrows at non-
game fish, such as gar and buffalo carp, and retrieve by crank-
ing the reel handle. He has become proficient at bow fishing
and has made it one of his favorite pastimes in his outdoors life.

During the time Tim worked as a fisheries technician,
strong friendships were developed. He worked with and
became friends of people like Rick Hill, Benjy Kinman, Kerry
Prather, Billy Mitchell and Tim Slone. All have been mainstays
of the Fish and Wildlife Department in Frankfort and have
grown to respect Tim, starting with the days when he did the
non-glamorous "grunt" jobs associated with being a fisheries
technician.

"Part of our work was to get vehicles and boats ready for

service," said co-worker Rick Hill, "and Tim was right there working with us, even with the disability."

Tim Farmer had progressed a long way since he stumbled, dumbfounded, up the embankment after wrecking his motorcycle in the summer of 1984. He had born physical pain and mental anguish. He endured a long period of adjustment to learn a new way of doing both routine activities, plus ones that required great effort and practice. He proved he could be a happy and viable force in the workplace, even excel and surpass some without disabilities. He might have stayed, content, as a fisheries technician for a very long time while raising his family and fishing and hunting in his spare time.

Tim might have, but the deep down restlessness in his heart, the Daniel Boone spirit, had started agitating him again.

42

GRAYSON Journal

Kentucky Publishing Company
dba/Journal Enquirer   USPS285-860

TWO SECTIONS — 24 PAGES

TUESDAY MORNING, JUNE 26

Cyclist Injured

Bystanders look over the scene of a motorcycle accident on Sunday afternoon that sent Tim Farmer, 20, of Rt. 3, Grayson to Cabell-Huntington Hospital. A spokesman for the Carter County Emergency Service said Farmer suffered serious damage to an arm, cuts, and lost a large amount of blood in the accident. The accident occurred shortly after 4 p.m. According to the Grayson Police Department, Farmer was apparently heading south on KY 1 and was trying to enter the ramp to the west bound lane of I-64 when he lost control of his motorcycle. The motorcycle struck the guard rail, throwing Farmer off the bike and over an embankment. Police officer Rick May said Farmer climbed up the bank and walked across Carol Malone Blvd. before anyone stopped to help.

Local newspaper coverage of Tim's motorcycle accident.
Photo compliments of *Grayson Journal-Times*

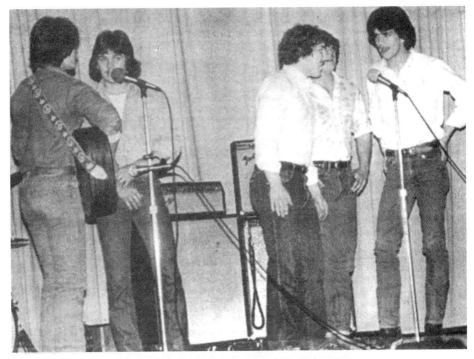

"Laid Back" was one of the more popular arts at the
Grayson Rotary Club Variety Show. The group played
tunes from country melody to rock and roll.

Tim (far right), the crooner, during his high school days.

Photo compliments of *Grayson Journal-Times*

44

WEDNESDAY MORNING, APRIL 18, 1979

East Captures Track Meets

By JOEY TRIMPER

Coach Jim Clark's East Carter Boys Tract Team won back-to-back triangular track meets April 10 and April 11.

Performing before the local fans Tuesday, East defeated teams from Greenup Co. and Lewis Co. The final scores were East 76, Greenup 57, and Lewis 34.

The East Carter victory was paced by individual winners O'Leary Haight, shot put (42' 6''); Dean Hall, high hurdles (16.6 sec) and discus (113' 8''); Rob Chaney, 440 yd. dash (52.5 sec.); Woody Dearfield, 880 yd. dash (2:17. min.); Lenny McDavid, long jump (17'

6'') and Paul Burnett, 2 mile run (11:15 min.). In addition to the individual winners, the mile relay team placed first with a time of 3:52 minutes.

At Morehead Wednesday, the Raiders had a closer battle, but still prevailed over University of Breckinridge and Whitesburg. East scored a winning total of 66 points, while Breck finished with 57 and Whitesburg 38.

Dean Hall repeated as a double winner, capturing the shot put (41' 6'') and the discus (114' 3''); Rob Chaney, 100 yd. dash (10.6 sec.); Van Baker, long jump (17' 10''); Tim Farmer, high jump (5' 4''); and Woody Dearfield, 440 yard run (56 sec.) captured first place in their events.

Congratulations ---
Our K Mart Employee
Part time-Mens Wear
Tim Farmer

"On the right track" for success.
Photo compliments of *Grayson Journal-Times*

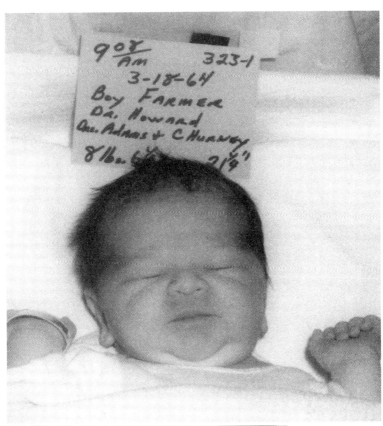

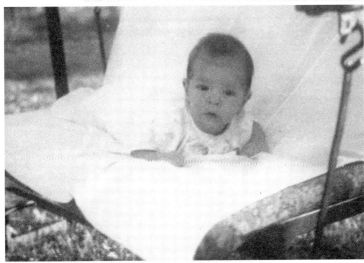

Is Tim Farmer
peering into the
TV camera?
Photos
compliments of
Jerry and Sherry
Farmer

Tim's favorite farm pond, a source of many happy childhood memories in Mason County. Photo compliments of Steve Flairty

Tim hands off on East Carter High's relay team.
Photo compliments of Jerry and Sherry Farmer

Five From East Headed For State Meet

Five members of the East Carter Track Team will be taking part in the state track meet.

The five earned the opportunity to advance by placing either first or second at the sectional track meet, held Saturday at Clay County.

Tim Farmer had the best individual finish, winning the 400 meter dash in a time of 51.35.

Farmer was also a member of East's winning 1,600 meter relay team. Farmer teamed up with Vince Thomas, Van Baker, and Rick Wilburn for a time of 3:32.39.

Gwen Snyder will be the only East girl in the state meet. She earned the trip by placing second in the 1,600 meter run.

East Carter High School track star.
Photo compliments of Jerry and Sherry Farmer

Tim's good friend, Phillip. They shared many adventures.
Photo compliments of Steve Flairty

Great-Granny Carr loved her flowers.
Photo compliments of Jerry and Sherry Farmer

Great-Granny Carr with
son, Ed (Tim's grandfather)
and a stringer of fish.
Photo compliments of Jerry
and Sherry Farmer

East Carter High School graduation picture, 1982.
Photo compliments of Jerry and Sherry Farmer
Photo by Hall's Photography, Stanton, Kentucky

"Locked and cocked" as a U.S. Marine.
Photo compliments of Jerry and Sherry Farmer

Family vacation. Tim in forefront, sister Deborah sitting and brother Jonathon held by father Jerry. Mother Sherry standing.
Photo compliments of Jerry and Sherry Farmer

Deborah and Tim.
Photo compliments of Jerry and Sherry Farmer

Tim's work as a sculptor.
Photo compliments of Steve Flairty

An example of Tim's artwork and appreciation for Native-American culture. The picture was painted as a teenager.
Photo compliments of Steve Flairty

Tim standing in front of Orangeburg Elementary in Mason County.
The school is now part of a junkyard.
Photo compliments of Steve Flairty

Tim found this skull as a 15-year-old, causing quite a stir.
Photo compliments of Jerry and Sherry Farmer

Sherry Farmer at home near Grayson, Kentucky.
Photo compliments of Steve Flairty

Jerry and Sherry Farmer outside their home near Grayson, Kentucky.
Photo compliments of Steve Flairty

(opposite) "Old School Predestination Baptist," constituted in 1908,
where Tim's father and mother attend. The church is located in
Denton, Kentucky.
Photo compliments of Jerry and Sherry Farmer

5

TV

In 1994, Dave Shuffett left America's oldest outdoor show, public TV's *Kentucky Afield,* to later host a program called *Kentucky Life.* The folks at Fish and Wildlife were now in the market for a new host to carry on the celebrated tradition. The job attracted a lot of interest, and many good candidates applied. They didn't have to look far to find the one they wanted, however. They chose 30-year-old fisheries technician Tim Farmer from among their own ranks.

"I had gained a lot of confidence working those years as a technician. It was a wonderful job, but I felt the need to step out, to be challenged again. Plus, my kids were growing up and they needed things," Tim said, "but really, the *Kentucky Afield* host was a job I thought I'd never get."

Fisheries biologist Kerry Prather, who hired Tim as a technician, was not surprised by the choice. He had spent a lot of time working beside him and knew his strengths. Prather considered Tim to be very solid in the needed skills for the program.

"Tim has always had lots of charisma. He knows how to get along with all kinds of people and he just has a real passion for the outdoors. Also, he never acted like he was above doing technician work all those years before he got the *Kentucky Afield* job."

Norm Minch, a supervisor for both Kentucky Afield TV and its magazine, was part of the hiring process. "Tim's never met a stranger. He can talk to anybody about any subject, especially the outdoors. We thought that would make a great personality for a TV show host. Plus, he's the type of person who always stops what he's doing to talk to people about the outdoors, especially those with disabilities."

Tim was not even sure he should apply at first, but lots of others who knew him gave him personal encouragement, plus they recommended him to the ones doing the hiring. Even with all the goodwill on his side, one friend said, "Tim Farmer pretty much just sold himself, with both his knowledge and his personality."

For Farmer, the early shows as host clearly highlighted his enthusiasm and intensity, but he was a bit nervous, even though he and friends had often done some of their own video filming in the outdoors before he got the new job. In fact, *The Outdoors Channel* had shown some interest in his work.

"I had been doing some things to practice for this type of thing when I had visited out west. Being put in front of a camera for the statewide show was pretty frightening at first," said Tim, "but now, after doing hundreds of segments over the years, it's no big problem today. I feel at ease."

Tim recalled the first show's final moments, when he was not sure of how he'd sign off. He was struggling. "Without much thought, I just said 'Hope to see you in the woods, or on the water'," explained Tim. That phrase has now become a trademark for all Tim's *Kentucky Afield* shows, highly recognizable to his many fans. He has also added the introductory phrase, "Join us as we journey across the commonwealth seeking adventure."

In fact, Tim enhances the connection with the audience and himself by often looking directly into the camera, pausing, and making a humorous aside comment or a revealing facial gesture–letting the viewers know that he doesn't take himself too seriously. In a 1998 turkey hunt in Robertson County, Tim zipped toward a turkey he had just shot. When he reached the animal, he rejoiced as a child might–with unabashed glee. Then, at the end of the program, viewers watched the farm owner pull the mud-stuck *Kentucky Afield* vehicle to solid ground—with Tim on camera sporting an impish grin. Viewers can always tell he's having fun and wants them to join him, too.

Harold Knight, of Knight and Hale Game Calls and *Knight and Hale's Ultimate Hunting Show* on *The Outdoors Channel*, is a big fan of Tim as the host of *Kentucky Afield*. "Tim is so relaxed, has lots of fun and is good to the people he has on the show. He lets the guests be the experts, but he is also very knowledgeable about the outdoors. The sky's the limit in how far Tim can go in his career."

Knight and Tim enjoy a jocular relationship. "After watching Tim use his mouth to crank the fishing reel, I told him I was gonna get him some chocolate on the handles. He's not sensitive at all about that kind of teasing." Tim, in tune with the joke, later told a hospital volunteer group that when he goes to look for a new reel, he chooses one by first doing a "taste test."

Knight, who has appeared on *Kentucky Afield* numerous times, raved about Tim's influence on others, saying that "lots of people have been inspired to try things they wouldn't normally have."

On the show, Tim is usually "in the woods or on the water," as viewers often hear him say. Most segments take place in Kentucky, where the state boasts the second greatest volume of running freshwater in America–behind only giant Alaska.

Take the uncountable numbers of tributaries that feed the main rivers, a legion of small farm ponds, and a still significant supply of woodland habitats friendly to a diverse game population and you have a great stage for the production of *Kentucky Afield*. Almost as important is Kentucky's colorful, soulful and proud people who interact with nature and each other every week as viewers often identify with them. These people help add seasoning to the stew, and Tim Farmer and the production crew stir the ingredients into a marvelously informative and entertaining outdoors program, one that touches viewers all across the land that so attracted woodsman icon, Daniel Boone.

The show offers a diversity of weekly features. And, though it has repeating types of hunting and fishing, they are made interesting by taking place at different sites, with different people, and often with different kinds of fishing gear or hunting weapons. Often, a different slant might be taken on a segment. For example, a squirrel hunting trip may emphasize the hunting dogs and their skills in "treeing" the animals rather than on the humans who are hunting. On a trip to Bath County in 2002, viewers were treated to the wonderful exploits of Billy Smith's squirrel dog, "Tiny." On another segment, Steve Fugate's waterfowl dog, "Cinco," provided a bit of comedy by trying to retrieve two ducks at the same time on a hunt in McCracken County. A bluegill fishing trip to Beaver Lake demonstrated that the lake still has lots of fish to catch, contrary to rumors otherwise.

The artistry and sport of fox hunting was shown in a trip to Shelby County. Viewers saw a blend of picturesque apparel, open country landscapes and a cultured tradition in the bluegrass. Though there was some voice over and a few interviews, the most important communication was done visually and was actually produced by Tim.

Always seeking variety, Tim introduced one show by announcing "Fish by the millions!" then demonstrated, on location at the Frankfort Fish Hatchery, the process whereby white and striped bass are cross-bred to produce a "hybrid" fish. Each step was shown clearly, with Tim allowing the experts to do the teaching and making sure to give them center stage. The time spent was an interesting, educational nugget that provided a break from the routine.

In an "almost all girls coon hunt" segment, Tim and a group of young ladies participated in an all night raccoon hunting expedition. It was Tim at his best, teasing and cajoling his guests and convincing hunt leader Jo Ann Mattox to do a coon call, plus admit to the time her coon dog caught a skunk. Then, as Tim so often does, he closed out the segment with a suggestion that they go and find something to eat.

Show fans are encouraged to send pictures of their own fishing and hunting successes on *The One that Didn't Get Away* segment. In a few recent segments, the idea was carried even further. A woman in Western Kentucky, given a rod and reel for a Mother's Day gift, promptly used the gear to catch the state record crappie. Tim interviewed her and her husband. He also interviewed a gentleman in Eastern Kentucky who was responsible for two state record fish.

Private fish and wildlife organizations, such as the *National Wild Turkey Federation*, are given opportunities to inform the public of their work. Periodic state-wide call-in shows, featuring Tim and other Fish and Wildlife recreation officials, help keep hunters and fishermen up-to-date on laws and regulations as well as offering timely general advice.

On occasion, *Kentucky Afield* goes on location outside the borders of Kentucky. One such show took viewers to the Tennessee Aquarium in Chattanooga, Tennessee to see workers preparing food, then feeding hundreds of freshwater fish. The great connection to Kentucky is that many of the fish are native to the state–fish that viewers see regularly on the program and in their local waters. At the show's outset, Tim posed as a tourist at the entrance to the Tennessee Aquarium, inviting the viewer in on the fun. Inside, a combination of good filming, good interviewing and a well-written script made for a highly interesting show originating south of Kentucky but appropriate to the state audience.

Whenever a relevant point can be made for the good of young people, *Kentucky Afield* tries to insert it, often with Tim's leading. A bow fishing expedition at Nolin Lake, a rousing success for both Tim and guest guide Walt Kloeppel, culminated with a conversation about how bow fishing is exciting for youngsters who get bored easily. The two agreed that teaching a young person to shoot bow and arrows for deer, and then have them sit in a stand for hours is impractical, even counter-productive, to using the outdoors as an engaging hobby. The two see bow fishing as the sport with more compelling action for kids.

Tim has a knack for choosing show guests that will be appreciated by the audience, are unique and bring a certain chemistry to the interaction. He stays away from those who have over-sized egos. "One guy called us and his exact words were, 'I'm the hottest thing on the lake, everybody wants me.' That pretty much disqualified him from the show," said Tim. "I do a pretty good job of feeling people out before I invite them on the program. We don't need people with big egos."

Department official Tim Slone marvels at the way Tim has grown into the show. "Tim's gotten very knowledgeable about the television business. He's good about bringing out the best in the people he interviews. You've got to ask the right questions. You've got to bring a person's personality out. A lot of outdoors show hosts are not that skilled. With Tim, everybody feels real comfortable. He understands that even short segments need to have stories in them," Slone said. "And, he's plenty capable of going to a bigger market if he ever wanted to."

If one wonders how ideas for the show come, just follow Tim around as he travels. "We may stop at a gas station some place and somebody will start talking to Tim about a particular fishing place or something. He'll make the contact and then we'll have it on the show. He knows people everywhere," Slone said.

A question sometimes asked is about the success rate of bagging game and catching fish on the show. It appears awfully good most of the time, doesn't it? Is that realistic, one might ask? Although there are *Kentucky Afield* segments that show dry runs, mostly viewers see lots of game and fish taken—right before their eyes. At times when there is little action, the production crew often can make use of the footage, even if only to show scenery. For the most part, though, the fishing and hunting on the show gets results.

"That's because the hunters and fishermen we work with are usually experts in their own area," said Tim. "They've hunted their woods and know what is there. They know their waters, their fish and what to use to catch them, so it shouldn't be a big surprise that we do so well on the show."

According to Slone, the audience for *Kentucky Afield* is not only who you think it would be–hunters and fishermen. "There are a lot of older folks who watch the show and don't hunt or fish. It's a part of Kentucky. It's a connection to their past, almost," Slone said.

Having them as a significant part of the viewers might have something to do with Tim Farmer's ability to relate to senior citizens. "I've seen older people invite Tim into their houses after only meeting him a few minutes before," said Slone. "They'll show him their antiques and things because he is easy to get to know."

Other viewers are professionals, women, the young and also, of course, people with disabilities. The show is likely to become even more important in the future because the number of active participants who hunt and fish in Kentucky is diminishing. The Fish and Wildlife Department is financed primarily by the buying of hunting and fishing licenses, which may necessitate staff cutbacks if the trend continues.

Kentucky Afield, hosted by Tim Farmer, is an important

vehicle for getting an important message to the public–that the joy of involving one's self in the great outdoors in Kentucky is important enough to support whole-heartedly. It is "something that benefits everybody, even people who don't get out and hunt or fish," said Slone.

The show also has provided Tim a platform to exhibit what is possible for those who have the determination to overcome their physical disabilities. Continually, viewers see a one-armed man do outdoor hobbies with excellence. He has fun, teaches and encourages. Almost makes you want to get up off the couch and *get active.*

6

Adaptations

S ome would liken life to a huge jigsaw puzzle, full of many irregularly shaped pieces. According to the metaphor, the pieces will find their interlocking partners, sometimes early in the process, sometimes later. As the puzzle nears completion, the individual pieces and their purposes are unveiled, producing "the big picture."

When pre-teen Tim Farmer chanced to see the one-armed man around Maysville, he would always take notice. Today, Tim recognizes the disabled man of his youth, in some respects, as a forerunner of his own future.

"I have vivid memories of riding backseat around town in our family's '69 gold Impala, and I would always take note of the one-armed man," said Tim. "He did yard work all around town. Today it would be called landscaping. I remember him lifting heavy things. He had a certain way of doing every-thing. I remember him putting his foot on the chain saw to start it. I would see him everywhere. He had a friendly face and lots of kids. He walked with a purpose and a dignity. The guy was working with chain saws, hand tools, hedge trimmers, lawn mowers. *He wasn't sitting down because he had only one arm."*

Was it just a coincidental item, like so many that come along at different times? You might have trouble convincing Tim Farmer that it's purely a coincidence. He believes that things happen for a reason. The one-armed man, though he, himself, was probably unaware, served as a model for seven-year-old Tim Farmer. Tim saw a guy, almost in a matter-of-fact way, adapt to circumstances beyond his control. Tim was inspired by the man's sparkling countenance, the way he carried himself and went about his business. In short, it's about attitude.

Tim believes that for those who have disabilities, it's all about making adaptations, or adjustments, so that life may continue with enjoyment and meaning. In fact, Tim would prefer to call disabilities something else–"aggravations."

"It shouldn't be a big issue. Rather than handicap or disability, I prefer to call it an aggravation," Tim said. "Take ironing, or making a pot of coffee. You spill it. You burn yourself. Like putting toothpaste on your toothbrush. There's a constant process of aggravation. It's infringing on my time, making things less immediate. Going out the door every morning, I have a cell phone, a cup of coffee and a planbook. I have to sit each on the floor. Then I have to take the same cell phone, the same cup of coffee and the same planbook and sit them on the door stoop. I lock the door. Then I pick each one up again and take them to the truck hood. Open the truck door. Pick up the coffee, sit it in the truck. Pick up the planbook, sit it in the truck. Pick up the cell phone, sit it in the truck. I get in the truck and start moving out my bumpy driveway (about a quarter mile long). I grab my coffee so it won't spill. As I hold it, I drive with my knee out to the highway. In other words, a lot has gone on before I get out on the road."

Not all people appreciate ones who have aggravations, however. "I had a co-worker, he's gone now, who took issue with me because I used to park as close to the office as I could because of all these little aggravations I have to deal with. It's not because I feel sorry for myself or make excuses. It was just to help make it a little easier. He had a hateful little mind."

The point Tim hopes to make is that even though it is real hard, one who possesses "aggravations" must make an ongoing mental adjustment to successfully do normal routines. The challenge may get even bigger when one seeks to stretch his reach to more adventurous items in life, like fishing and hunting.

"But I've got nothing compared to somebody, say, who is in a wheel chair," said Tim. "I'm not feeling sorry for myself because there is always somebody who has a worse aggravation than me."

Tim, almost to a fault, refrains from seeking direct help in doing his activities. He wants others to see independence in action, plus he'd rather not burden others. There are some exceptions, though, in special situations. "When I'm on vacation and out on the ocean fishing, I want every second to count. If someone wants to help me put some bait on the hook so I can get lines in the water quicker, I'm totally fine with that. Sometimes when we're out at a pond fishing with night-crawlers, I let people help. I'm still learning how to use a bait holder, but right now that isn't working out real well."

Randell Gibson is a fun-loving, honest, don't-feel-sorry-for-me kind of a guy who loves fishing and enjoys helping others to help themselves. That's why it shouldn't be a surprise that he quickly hit it off with Tim Farmer.

An award-winning fishing guide from the Burkesville, Kentucky, area, Gibson examined a piece of adaptive fishing gear that Tim was using and clearly found that it just wasn't working. "It was some kind of a small, wooden apparatus that only helped him reel in small fish. Tim asked to pick my brain about it," said the burley outdoorsman. "I thought about it a while, then took some 80 schedule pvc pipe and made some modifications on it. Now Tim has been able to catch 50-60 lb. flatheads and has fished in saltwater with the contraption."

The adaptive pipe is attached at the waist and holds the rod and reel out in front of Tim without his needing to stabilize it with his left hand. A strap around the neck adds further stabilization, especially for larger fish. It allows, however, for him to use his hand to reel the line in. Without the rod holder, he would need to use his teeth to reel in, making it practically impossible to get bigger fish into the boat.

"With this to help me, I've caught fish as small as bluegills and as big as sharks," said Tim.

Tim uses a fly rod with a push-button, automatic reel without the pole stabilizer. He occasionally uses a spin-casting reel without the stabilizer and simply cranks the handle with his teeth.

When Tim talks about people who have helped him most in making mechanical or equipment adjustments for his disability, Gibson is always mentioned. "Randell is really good at figuring out how to make things work, a real smart guy," said Tim. "He's helped a lot of other people with disabilities who want to enjoy the outdoors, too." Gibson has been on about a dozen *Kentucky Afield* episodes. He is also one of Tim's best friends in the hunting and fishing world.

Tim's father Jerry, a retired civil engineering designer, produced for his son a board mounted vice grip pliers, which could be steadied by leg or foot. It was used as an extra hand to hold a hook steady while being baited or tied onto the fishing line. The adaptation has since been revised by Tim's friend, Chris Breeding, to make it portable with the ability to be strapped on a leg.

"I see a lot of good folks out there everyday. There are always people stepping forward to help another overcome physical barriers. Then, someone comes along afterward to make those adaptations even better. Sometimes, it's those who were helped first who later supply the improvements," Tim said.

The shooting appendage, or tab, in the middle of Tim's bowstring is quite simple, but crucial, to his ability to be a marksman archer. With a lot of use, the leather piece normally lasts only a few months. Recently, he has switched to braided nylon, which lasts longer. That brings up an obvious question. The tab for the bowstring can be easily replaced, but what about the wear and tear on Tim's teeth?

"I use only my left-side molars (jaw teeth)," said Tim, "and so far I haven't had any real trouble. Sometimes they can get a little sore if I shoot a lot over a real short time."

Co-worker Bill Mitchell worked along side Tim as they did repair and maintenance work on machinery and equipment, a part of their duties as fisheries technicians. The work was not as fun as such activities as gill-netting and electro-fishing. It often meant being down on their backs, with loads of grease on their face and hands.

"Tim had amazing speed for just using one hand. He would always stop and study about the way he would do something, then do it. He didn't ask for a lot of help, but he was not hard-headed about it when he needed it. Tim knew when certain things would require the help of another person, and then he'd ask."

Through continual use, Tim's left arm became very strong. That strength allowed him to shoot a rifle or shotgun by resting it briefly on his right shoulder. Through lots of practice, starting with a light-weight air rifle not long after the accident, he became both accurate and quick, able to hit live, flying birds or clay pigeons.

Tim uses a headset phone while driving. He has also learned the art of steering with his knees, which he uses on occasion. For Tim, a little technology, a lot of human ingenuity and some simple common sense combine to make his days be quite productive. And, he expects more ways to be found for people like him, with similar "aggravations," to make life more meaningful.

7

Service

With the exposure Tim Farmer receives on *Kentucky Afield* and on public appearances, he attracts the interest of many people who have experienced their own disability. For these people, individuals who may have lost a limb and often in the prime of their lives, Tim is a model, a blueprint, for happier and more productive times. It is a role that he embraces, one that gives him another reason to roll out of bed in the morning.

Jenny Wurzback knows Tim from his work with Cardinal Hill Hospital in Lexington. "I saw him spend just a little time with a young lady who had lost full use of an arm. He had her shooting a bow using her mouth in no time. It was truly remarkable the difference it made in her self-esteem. On the same day, Tim talked to another of our patients about how he could make adaptations and continue to fish. The man's wife later told me that meeting Tim Farmer totally changed his outlook on everything. Tim is just so easy to be around and has such an effect on others," she said.

Jenny also related the work Tim has done for Cardinal Hill's Annual Game Dinner, one in which his band, *The Big Black Cadillacs,* has performed. "One of the fund-raising items was a fishing trip with Tim Farmer. I bought one just so my son could be around him," she said.

Tim has a natural ability to relate to kids. April Marcum, of Shriners Hospital, Lexington, remembers how children with prosthetic devices showed Tim how to tie shoes. Tim played along with them as a bungler. They thought it was humorous that he often showed up to mentor them wearing either cowboy boots or flip-flops on his feet.

"The kids told Tim it 'was easy and he should try it'," said Marcum.

Tim has worked with Shriners Hospital to mentor children who have loss of limb challenges. He has helped at "Prosthetic Camp," held at the Fish and Wildlife Game Farm and has presented his adaptive techniques at the hospital.

"Also, Tim has never refused us when we have called him to work with individual children," said Marcum. "I think he could have been a very good school teacher."

There is a message that Tim carries *wherever* he goes to talk to others. What does he tell those who have fallen into a sense of despondency over, say, losing a limb or other physical challenge that forces a dramatic life change?

Tim's answer is to the point. "The sky's still blue, food still tastes good, and if they go to Spain, it's going to look the same with one arm as two. Get active and set goals. If you're active, you're not going to be sitting on the couch feeling sorry for yourself. For me, life's a big playground. I always look for ways to enjoy it. "

People who want to see life that way, too, are anxious to talk with Tim about how that might come about. "I get phone calls all the time from people all over the country," Tim said, "They want to know how they can continue doing an outdoor activity they love."

Very often, those who ask for advice want to find out how to shoot a bow by pulling the string back with their mouth. One who recently sought out Tim's expertise is Chris Breeding, who lost the use of his right arm the same way Tim did–by a motorcycle accident near his home. In Chris's situation, home is in Dry Ridge, Kentucky. Breeding has followed the lead of Tim in the attire he wears on his right arm, a long sleeve shirt and a glove to cover his hand. "Keeps it from getting banged up because it just kind of flails around," Breeding said matter-of-factly. With the confidence he has gained recently, Breeding is considering getting back into riding a specially adapted motorcycle. He already has reclaimed his regular hunting and fishing activities, though, he laughed, "I haven't gotten any better at it."

On this sunny April afternoon at the Game Farm in Frankfort, where bow shooters participated in the *Tim Farmer Archery Classic* competition, Breeding exhibited a high skill level while shooting aside his mentor. Both talked about their similarities in experience, such as how they both have opportunities to answer a lot of questions from others. By talking to each other, they also found a mutual understanding of the pain level they live with constantly, something they realize will probably not go away. Chris is becoming very much like his friend Tim.

"Chris has also become a big help to me," Tim emphasized, "and in the *Overcoming Physical Barriers Workshop* program we do, Chris helps others who are participating. He is a good trouble-shooter for problems that need fixed there." The workshop is designed for participants to learn about techniques and equipment to help then more fully enjoy outdoor recreation, particularly archery, hunting and fishing.

Tim, unlike Chris, has no desire to ride motorcycles any longer, preferring to stick with hunting and fishing.

Jason Maxedon, a forestry biologist from western Tennessee, is another person who has profited from Tim's bow shooting help. Maxedon, in his early thirties, lost an arm in a farm equipment accident. He traveled to Kentucky to get help from Tim. Now, with the coaching, he can shoot one-handed quite easily. "Jason was shooting very accurately in less than an hour," Tim said.

Ben Brown is a 23-year-old Navy veteran, who, like Tim, acquired a disability from a motorcycle. Ben was near the same age that Tim was when he had his accident. He is confined to a wheelchair but is figuring out a way to do things outdoors. He gets an upbeat frame of mind from what he has seen Tim do after meeting him at a fund-raising game dinner for Cardinal Hill Hospital in 2004.

"It's amazing to me all the things Tim can do even though he has his disability," said Ben. "He inspires me to get out and do things, too." Brown recently did most of the work in building a deck for his home. He thinks there will come a time when he will be able to do all of the work on similar projects.

All told, Tim has helped individuals from Michigan, Texas, Wisconsin, Arkansas, Alabama, and Georgia, as well as Kentucky and Tennessee to participate in archery despite the loss of a limb. Probably uncountable are individuals he helps almost daily in other adaptive hunting and fishing techniques, plus the many TV viewers who see him weave his magic every week.

Tim is philosophical about the opportunities he has for service every day. "One day it hit me why I had the accident," he said. "I feel I'm part of a plan that wouldn't be without what happened to me. I take it very seriously."

His brother, Jonathan, who is in the U.S. Army, gave an indication of Tim's capacity to care. "The night I left for Iraq, he drove for five or six hours—a one-armed man came to help me carry my bags into the airport. He was upset and wanted to know if they needed a one-armed ex-Marine over there, too. Tim is fiercely patriotic and wants to be part of the action."

Schools and scouting groups often ask Tim to share his story and a word of encouragement. He does so when his schedule allows it. When it is practical, he carries his bow along and wows the audience. Speaking and demonstrating his mouth shooting before a group of senior citizens, he was presented a large print of a wildcat. A person in the audience quipped, "Don't kill that thing, Tim!"

Chances to share with groups abound, but he has to be careful not to overdo it. "I'd love to go even more, but if I accepted every speaking invitation, I'd have no time to do anything else," he said. As mentioned earlier, that's a big reason he agreed to do the book. He hopes that more people can be lifted up and, in turn, they can go and encourage others.

8

Music

It was Saturday evening, late April in rural Owen County. Out in the clear, crisp air, the redbuds' blooms were fading but the dogwoods were dressed in stunning whites, as if a big doins' was about to commence nearby.

On the curvy side road #3103, the newly built Brown Hall's parking lot was starting to fill one hour before the grand opening of the Kentucky Jamboree. The show had been moved from its Georgetown location to the 300-acre Jackie Robinson farm, called "Home 'n the Hills," headquarters of the nationwide traveling musicians, The Robinson Family.

The special guests that night were baritone Arnett Stratton and Elvis Presley, *a.k.a. Tim Farmer, Kentucky Woodsman.*

No one knew how many people would come to a place so far out in the country, but as patrons steadily walked through the door, it was apparent that they saw the need to head on in to the stage area to secure a seat.

By the time the starting time of 7:30 had come,

Jamboree officials were "going to have more chairs brought in," as host Jackie Robinson stated it. By the time the ribbon had been cut and community leaders and politicians spoke on this very special occasion, Brown Hall was packed with upwards of 300 paying customers.

Tim received nice applause when he was introduced as host of *Kentucky Afield*, and after the audience heard him deliver strong performances of *You Don't Know Me* and the old gospel standard, *Peace in the Valley*, the hootin', hollerin' and hand clapping picked up. They quickly found out that Tim Farmer can do more than chase rabbits and catch fish. He quickly won them over. But the real treat was in the second half of the show. Tim did a foot stompin', body riveting Elvis rendition. The crowd went wild and Jackie Robinson blurted, "That was the price of admission, everything else is free."

Anyone watching the Kentucky Jamboree that night could see that Tim Farmer has a load of musical talent. It wasn't an impromptu, Johnny-come-lately kind of thing, though. Tim and his music experience started a long time ago, when as a small child in Georgetown, Kentucky, he participated in a "band" with sister Debbie and some neighborhood children.

"They used garbage can tops for cymbals, barrels and some toy instruments. They were wonderful and they serenaded people all over the Warrendale area," said Sherry Farmer.

The first item Tim ever bought with his childhood allowance was an Elvis record, *Are You Lonesome Tonight?* Today he calls it "the best Elvis song ever recorded." In his younger days, Tim also enjoyed mixing a little Elvis Presley music into his religion.

"Our family traveled all around to religious meetings when I was a kid," said Tim. "When I was sitting in the back seat of the car as a real young boy, feeling hot as a grease ball, Dad and Mom would have the AM radio station on, listening to religious programs. Every now and then, an Elvis gospel song would come on. I remember hearing Elvis sing *How*

Great Thou Art and the hair was standing up on my neck. I had never heard gospel music like that."

Tim also watched gospel music on the black and white TV as his parents were getting ready for church, with groups such as The Florida Boys performing. "Even then, I felt like I could recognize good harmony as well as bad. There was such an innocence about the music I heard when I was little. I still like that simple, sentimental kind of music today." You can take a trip with Tim in his pick-up, and you'll hear that kind of music on most of his CD's.

According to his parents, music might even rival the great outdoors as a true passion of Tim Farmer.

"Music might even be a greater passion," Tim responded. "But the accident kind of curtailed my professional plans a bit."

During his year in the military hospitals after the accident, Tim often listened to classical music on his tape player. It helped him keep settled mentally and emotionally. "I listened to *The Academy of Ancient Music*. Water music, baroque. I would lose myself in that stuff."

His taste for classical music didn't suddenly crawl into bed in the confines of a hospital room, however. "I listened to classical music in my room when I was a kid. I liked the music that reminded me of a pastoral setting and I liked the music of a storm coming and leaving. My favorite was *The Pastoral Symphony*, Beethoven's 6th Symphony. It was so visual," Tim said. "Mom liked to listen to it, too. We got the *Time-Life* series of music. She liked Chopin and I liked Beethoven. I could always envisage the scene I heard in the music."

Jerry Farmer told about showing Tim a few chords on his guitar at a very early age. "He picked it up very quickly," Jerry said, "and then he pretty much taught himself the guitar and other instruments. He just had a knack for understanding music." Jerry's father, Harlan, was also a great music lover and gave Tim his first guitar and amplifier. Tim called Grandpa

Farmer a "great guy and he encouraged me a lot."

Tim remembered taking piano lessons as a youngster. The experience was not pleasant. "I took lessons from a lady at her house near Maysville. When I made mistakes, she'd crack me over the knuckles with a pencil. It really turned me off. I decided then that if I was going to learn music, I'd do it by myself."

When Tim was not out in the woods, he often could be found alone in his bedroom, tinkering for hours with his music. As he progressed in knowledge, he also began to meet with music-minded friends to arrange music. Naturally, with Tim involved, it produced a bit of adventure.

"It was late one night and Sherry and I had already gone to bed," said Jerry. "Tim and his friends had spent hours working on a special song arrangement. Tim woke us up and insisted that we hear it, so we took the time to listen. What they had done was absolutely beautiful."

"Everyone in that little group was so excited. The interesting thing is that one of that group went on to play with Billy Ray Cyrus," Sherry said.

Tim also was a high school classmate and played a little music with Dean Hall, son of country music star Tom T. Hall. Dean later appeared with his band on *Kentucky Afield*.

To this day, Tim gravitates toward the "old," disdaining today's "faster" music, according to brother Jonathan. You'd think that high-octane Tim would like to rev it up on the heavy metal, wouldn't you?

"The slow music of old has a calming effect on Tim," said Jonathan, who confesses that he "stole" some of Tim's music when they were kids.

After high school and before he joined the Marines, Tim played music in and around Grayson. "At that time, playing music had actually become my livelihood for a few years," he said. "Mom wasn't too crazy about some of the places I played, though."

His parents believe that in the absence of the motorcycle accident, music might well have been his chosen career.

Though Tim is primarily a guitarist, he plays the keyboard and drums, as well as being a vocalist, which he does for his band, The Big Black Cadillacs.   Much of the music the band plays are "oldies" from the fifties through the seventies. One can get another sense of his musical taste by noticing the background music on *Kentucky Afield,* mostly thumb pickin' guitar in the style of Merle Travis and Chet Atkins.

Bennie Judd, a member of the group, is impressed with what Tim has to offer musically. "Tim has more talent with just one arm than most have with two," Judd said.

One of Tim's pickin' buddies, Eddie Pennington, is amazed with how "Tim can do the different parts of harmony arrangements like few can." Pennington, who supplies most of the background music for *Kentucky Afield,* also praised Tim's "young Elvis" rendition he does frequently on stage. "Lots of people do Elvis, but not many have Elvis's voice down as a young person like Tim does," he said.

Tim developed his Elvis voice pretty much the way he always masters new and difficult skills–by immersing himself in what he is doing and endless repetition. "As a young boy, I would sit and listen to Elvis records over and over, mouthing the words until it became totally natural," he explained.

Motivated by music's importance to his own life, Tim is in the talking stages of a way to showcase young musical talent from Kentucky. He hopes to bring live performances of such to the stage–where many can watch and appreciate.

He is also formulating plans to start a "more technical, jazz big band."

"I can feel the whole music thing sucking me in," said Tim. "Since the accident, it has lain dormant for a long while. I can feel the pull, much like it was with the hunting and fishing a few years ago."

Tim conquers the forces of evil...
Photo compliments of Scott Hayes

Tim and daughter Rebekah enjoy the *Star Wars* premier in Lexington.
Photo compliments of Scott Hayes

Tim changes shirts for a gig at Carter Caves State Park.
Photo compliments of Scott Hayes

Tim relaxes in his pick-up truck.
Photo compliments of Scott Hayes

First day to meet Katie,
Tim's English Pointer, 1995.
Photo compliments of Tim Farmer

Tim with beard.
Upper Peninsula,
Canada, 2002.

Photo compliments of
Tim Farmer

Dolphin fishing, Marathon Key, 2004.
Photo compliments of Tim Farmer

43" muskie caught in Buckhorn Lake, 2003.
Photo compliments of Tim Farmer

Black bear archery kill. Approximately
450 lbs., Ontario, Canada, 2004.
Photo compliments of Tim Farmer

Walt Kloeppel with bonnethead shark, 1999.
Photo compliments of Tim Farmer

(opposite page) Tim with turkey, Greenup County, 2002.
Photo compliments of Tim Farmer

Tim demonstrates
shooting a bow
with his mouth at
Shriner's Hospital
for Children,
Lexington,
Kentucky.
Photo compliments
of April Marcum

Tim Farmer and
Randell Gibson
with turkeys, 1995.
Photo compliments
of Tim Farmer

Shark on! Florida
Keys, 1999.
Photo compliments of
Tim Farmer

Tim, before dawn on a turkey
hunt in Greenup County.
Photo compliments of Steve Flairty

Tim's daughters, Rebekah and Elizabeth, 2001.
Photo compliments of Jerry and Sherry Farmer

Tim, bow fishing for gar.
Photo compliments of Tim Farmer

Reeling one in.
The Keys, 1998.
Photo compliments of Tim Farmer

Tim practices his music at home. Photo compliments of Jerry and Sherry Farmer

Elizabeth and Tim enjoy a nice catch. Photo compliments of Tim Farmer

Check out these choppers, 2004.
Photo compliments of Tim Farmer

Georgia archery wild boar hunt, 2004.
Photo compliments of Tim Farmer

Helping withdraw arrows at the *Tim Farmer Archery Classic* in Frankfort, Kentucky.
Photo compliments of Steve Flairty

Tim with Shawn Henyce.
Photo compliments
of Steve Flairty

Tim outside one of his favorite Frankfort eateries.
Photo compliments of Steve Flairty

Chris Breeding and Tim
shoot some arrows.
Photo compliments
of Steve Flairty

Tim with Billy Jarboe with some good eatin' walleye.
Green River Lake, 2003.   Photo compliments of Tim Farmer

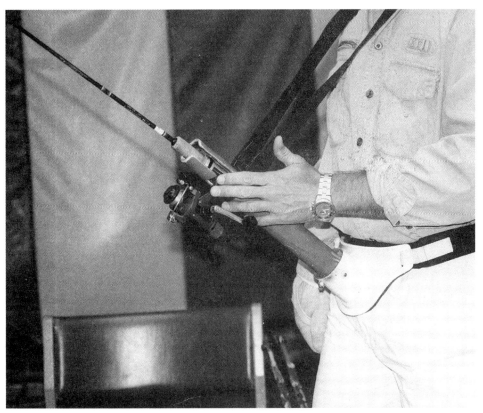

Tim's fishing apparatus, used to stabilize pole while he reels
with his left hand.
Photo compliments of April Marcum

(opposite page) Roger Singleton and Triple Crown winning jockey
Steve Cauthen share a laugh with Tim at the premier of *Seabiscuit*.
Photo compliments of Scott Hayes

9

Youth

The youthful life experiences of Tim Farmer, as one looks back, showed early that his approach to living would truly be an engaging one. Tim as a youngster was wide-eyed, positive and always seeking adventure. He continually pushed outward the barriers that might keep him from enjoying his own little world. He didn't run roughshod over others, though. He was a charmer, and still is. You might say he had the spunk of Huck Finn but the love and nurturing family of the Waltons to soften him. By all accounts, it was a happy youth.

He was born in Louisville on March 18, 1964, the middle child between his sister Debbie, the oldest, and Jonathan, the youngest.

"Growing up with my parents was no stress. Dad was good. Mom was good. Everything was taken care of. I can still see me getting my bath, washing my hair and sitting on the floor in front of the fan drying it. I feel kind of guilty sometimes when I see people who had unhappy childhoods. Mine was wonderful," he said.

The family moved to Georgetown in 1967, where Jerry worked on a degree at Georgetown College. There, Tim attended Garth Elementary School and "did well," said his mother. She also remembered Tim as a small-time garbage scavenger.

"Timmy had a little friend and they did everything together. One day they brought all kinds of discarded things home that they found in the dumpsters around the neighborhood. They were so proud of all that junk they found. He just couldn't believe that people would throw such nice things away," she laughed.

Then, in 1970, the Farmers moved near Maysville and Tim thrived around what seemed a boundless wilderness area. The "woodsman" began to emerge in the rural Mason County countryside where he now lived.

Sherry Farmer recalled an event that must seem today to be symbolic of her son's life. "I can still see this moment in my mind. It was when Tim was about 10," explained Sherry. "Timmy picked up his BB gun and got his dog, "Patches (a cross between a beagle and a cocker spaniel)," along side him. He looked at me and said 'Mom, I'm goin' huntin.' I can still see him and that dog walking away towards the woods."

"When you're a kid in Mason County and you're the only one around the house except for your sister, it gets pretty boring," said Tim. "All day long, if I wasn't fishing I'd be off happy and doing things in the woods. All summer long, all fall long. I watched the ground squirrels, the sparrows, foxes. It taught me stealth for future hunting. I learned all the plants and trees. If I couldn't figure something out about nature myself, I'd ask and find out."

Father Jerry built the house on Olivet Church Road, near what is today's *Double A Highway.* That location was the staging ground for Tim's Daniel Boone-like adventures. His father also stayed actively involved with Tim, his older sister Deborah, and, later, younger brother Jonathan.

"Dad would take us out and let us see the power of a storm," Tim said. "Sitting up on a hill like we did, we could see tornadoes come up and we watched the wind swirl around. We'd wear plastic bags on our heads to protect us."

Tim also helped his mother in the garden, doing chores like picking and "breaking beans," and he *loved* her carrot cake at Christmas time. He watched his dog, Patches, dig deep in the soil for field mice and enjoyed catching water snakes on the bank of the pond. He also remembered crossing the bridge to Aberdeen, Ohio, to attend drive-in movies.

"We'd take some popcorn and sandwiches. We watched movies like *The Ten Commandents, How the West was Won, The Cowboys* and some of the Jerry Lewis movies."

He also found time to do a lot of fun reading all throughout his elementary years. "I read everyone of the Hardy Boys books. Also Louis L'Mour and S.E. Hinton's *The Outsiders*. I even read *Moby Dick*, the long version," he said. More recently, he has read, naturally, Allan Eckert's *The Frontiersman*.

But one should not make the mistake of thinking Tim was a quiet bookworm who caused teachers no trouble, particularly in the small, rural elementary school at Orangeburg, in Mason County. He was actually hyperactive and got bored easily—a sure-fire catalyst for creating his own brand of excitement, and he usually did.

"When I was in the third grade, I remember vividly sitting in class thinking about climbing out the window and fishing at several different ponds in the area. I had it planned that I would get home about the time school was out," Tim said, "but I never acted on my impulses."

Are we talking about Tom Sawyer or Huck Finn?

Tim told of the time he was the ring-leader of a food throwing fight in the school cafeteria. "It was in the early seventies, when paddling was still being done," he said. "Our principal got me out in front of everybody in the cafeteria and whacked me hard. I probably deserved it."

It was a time period nationally that was rife with race issues. Tim talked about an incident that happened in his little corner of the world.

"We had one African-American student who had been placed at our small, rural school. He was very angry about it. In fact, he had a lot of issues. It was terrible for that particular kid, taking him out of where he was and putting him a different environment," Tim said. "I sat by him on the bus one day because everybody was being hateful to him."

Tim recalled the conversation they had.

"What are you doing sitting here?" asked the student.

"Nothing," Tim answered.

"Here, you want a drink of my pop?" said the student in a surly manner.

Tim accepted the drink and took a nice long swig, then handed the bottle back. The act left the student with a shocked look on his face.

"Man, I can't believe you did that," said the student.

Tim related how the two became friends after that small, seemingly unimportant incident. In the context of the early seventies, it was probably a bit unusual that a rural, white kid would "drink after" a black classmate.

Tim actually liked Orangeburg Elementary School a lot, especially when the traveling shows that performed before the student body came. He remembers a marionette, or puppet, show that still intrigues him as he thinks about it today. His fondest memories, though, are of a rootin', tootin' wild west show.

"The guy who came to our school was a cowboy who did shooting tricks and just about everything else, and it was a lot of fun," he said.

Then there was his favorite teacher, Mrs. Harrison, who taught Tim in the sixth grade. "She was kind of harsh, but she loved me," he remembered, "I got a lot of spankings from her.

She would catch me doing things I shouldn't, and she'd say, 'Farmer, I'm going to crown you into Gloryland. Get to the cloakroom!' Then she would whack me three times."

Recently, while looking over the now deserted and privately owned school building, he reminisced about the steep, concrete entrance steps. "We were having a special doings at the school and we were asked to bring some food. I brought what mom had made for me and ended up dropping it on those steps."

Not far from the school and still thriving is the Stone Lick Baptist Church, a place his father, a minister, once directed services. "I can remember spending a lot of hours in that church. There was no air conditioning and it was hard when somebody was speaking or praying and they 'got the blessing.' That meant that they would just keep on talking or praying," he grinned. "When they were blessed, we were cursed. As a kid, I wanted to be outside doing things."

He also remembered traveling southward to Alabama and Georgia with his parents to attend church-related "association" meetings. "I would look at the flora and fauna and turn over rocks outside the buildings," said Tim. "I actually believe a lot of times I got a lot better appreciation of the Creator by doing that than being in church."

There were camping trips to Florida that were memorable. "Some of my best memories were when we were camping in Florida. Every trip we took revolved around nature for me. I loved the smell of the tent, the canvas. It wasn't like the polyester kind today. When other kids were playing with some kind of toy, I was exploring, turning over rocks and looking at the trees. I felt there was a presence, something bigger, to nature. Being out there was almost like having my own cathedral."

When Tim was basking in the joys of outside adventure, there was an element of his natural surroundings that never failed to fascinate him. He loved the intoxicating sound and smell of a creek.

"I remember going places with my grandfather where it seemed there was always a creek. There was the smell of fishing worms in a can, too. I have vivid memories of those times. I can still remember many of the fish I caught, and I can still remember ones I didn't catch," he said. "I would lay in bed and agonize over those things."

Jerry told a story about a dead hawk that he brought home to show the family. "Tim was totally fascinated by that hawk. For a while, he took that animal wherever he went. He would lay it out and spread its wings, noticing carefully every part of it and studying it. Finally, after several days, I had to tell him to get rid of it. It was stinking so bad."

In 1977, the Farmer family moved eastward to the Carter County countryside, where Sherry and Jerry still reside. Like Mason County, it was pure heaven for Tim, now 13-years-old and continuing to crave adventure. A vast woodlands area rose steeply behind the family's house. It became his playground. It was a step up in nature exploration, according to Tim.

"I graduated from hickory and cedar to hemlock and oak when I moved to Carter County," he said. "I would explore my area of the woods a little at a time. Branch to branch, hill to hill. I remember walking down into this valley and looking at the hardwoods and seeing a little log cabin. There was a spring coming up out of the side of a hill. I'd just sit there and take it in. My hundred acres from Mason County had expanded in Carter County. Since that time, I think most of the major decisions in my life were made out in the woods, though not all were the right ones."

The community around small town Grayson was also the place where he met a new buddy, Phillip Green. Smallish but not afraid to try things, Phillip also enjoyed the life of the outdoors and didn't mind getting into a bit of boyish mischief with Tim.

Phillip talked about one hunting trip that resulted in more trouble than it was worth. "Not long after Tim had his motorcycle accident and came back here, we went hunting behind his parents' place. Tim wanted to show how he could still shoot things even with one arm. There was an old truck out there in the woods, which we shot at before we really got to huntin,' then we got to chasin' a deer. We got lost out there and ended up walking 11 miles before we got to a road and was able to call Tim's sister to pick us up."

Larry Thompson was along when Tim's natural curiosity almost brought about a disaster. It happened when the two went exploring and stumbled onto a treasure, namely a human skull. It appeared as Tim stuck his hand far back into the dark crevice of a local Carter County cave to retrieve what he thought was nothing out of the ordinary.

"Larry and I were wandering around in a beautiful area around Tygarts Creek. There was this huge waterfall and bluff with ferns, rhododendron and hemlock. Just gorgeous. There were all kinds of little caves and holes, and I was curious and crawled back into one of them. I reached for something back in there that first felt like pottery. I had pulled out a human skull! It was adventure, buddy…Then I yelled to Larry, 'Get over here, get over here.'"

In all the excitement of the finding, the two almost forgot it was getting dark. The temperature was getting colder, they were on strange land and it was a good three mile walk home. With the human skull under Tim's parka, they headed on down the gravel road and back to the main highway.

"Here we were walking down the highway, cold and it was getting dark. Then this guy pulls up behind us in a blue van. He asked us if we needed a ride, so we got in the van. Along the way, he asked us what I was carrying. First, I told him it was a rabbit. He asked again in a rough voice and told me I got it on *his* property. Then I told him what it really was. He dropped us off and didn't say much."

Mom, for sure, wanted to know what 15-year-old Tim was carrying.

"I pulled the skull out and Mom really reacted to it," Tim said. "We looked at it more closely and pulled out a couple of arrowheads from the cavity. This guy had been shot by two arrows and we talked about how he might have ended up back in that hole. Was he dragged into there after being killed? Could it have been him, being injured, crawling into that space to die? I've heard of people staying alive for a while with rods in their heads, so you never know...."

Sensing that this might be a significant finding, Tim decided to do what he called "responsible." He got in touch with Morehead State University about his archaeological discovery. Someone there informed a Huntington TV station, and a highly motivated reporter visited Grayson to interview Tim.

"That was my first time on TV," Tim said. "At school, I became "The Skull Man."

The reporter called again. This time he wanted to do a follow-up on the story. Against the best wishes of Tim's parents, who had received threatening calls from the landowners, the reporter and Tim sneaked back to the area and filmed a short follow-up piece. It must have made the owners mad, Tim figured, because of what happened next.

"PR (another friend), Larry and myself went back to the cave to explore some more. I just couldn't get enough of it. I was back in the cave digging up some pieces of flint and looking outside, when I saw a .30-30 rifle pointing to the ground, boots and a pair of jeans that weren't Larry's or PR's. I could see that it was the landowner and this was a pretty serious situation. I knew I'd have to turn on the charm, so I crawled out of the cave. Immediately, PR just took off like a rabbit, but Larry stayed."

"I thought I told you all not to come back up here," said the landowner, sternly.

"Man, we were just so excited and all, and...We apologize, we just had to get back up here," Tim said in the most good-natured way he could muster.

"Ya wanna dig, get back in there and dig," the man said roughly. Tim wasn't sure what the man meant, or what he was planning, if anything.

Tim crawled back into the cave, both scared and excited, and resumed his digging. In a short while, the man brought closure to the incident.

"Get the h--- out of here and don't come back," he said. Now there was no doubt the owner meant it.

Larry and Tim meekly obliged and that, finally, was enough adventure at that location for a while.

"We were not real thrilled about all the publicity," Sherry mentioned. "since Tim actually found the skull on another person's property."

Tim's father later took what might have been a good museum piece back to where it was found. Jerry sketched and still has diagrams of the archaelogical find of his son. Not finding out about the landowner with the gun until much later, Tim's mother was originally concerned about something else Tim could have pulled out of the crevice.

"Timmy worried me to death about picking up a snake with his hands," she said. "Nothing ever seemed to bother him, though." The little matter of the gun did matter to Tim, however, and definitely would have been very scary for his mother if she had been told at the time.

Tim's folks still possess two art pieces that show the appreciation he's always had for local American Indian culture. They are a painting and a small head sculpture he did as a young person.

There are more stories to tell. Phillip remembers the "albino frog incident" in which Tim and him were involved.

"Tim and I went frog giggin' one time and we brought the frogs we got down in the basement to prepare 'em. We made a mess and we used bleach to clean the floor. Some of the frogs got loose and a few days later we found one all white with bleach. It was an 'albino frog', all right."

The two friends even tried their hand at America's free enterprise system when Tim and Phillip started a "painting and wall-papering business."

"We had cards printed up and everything. I was a 'one-armed paper-hanger'," laughed Tim. The venture was short-lived, however, when Phillip accidentally kicked a bucket of paint onto a client's new carpet.

Tim and Phillip first met on the field of athletic endeavor, or, more specifically, out along the roadside as each trained for the East Carter High School track and cross country teams. Tim was a sprinter on the track team, Phillip a cross-country runner.

"One day I was out running cross country for practice and I saw this guy on the side of the road all balled up and in pain," Phillip said. "I later found out it was Tim Farmer, who was on our track team. I think he had a bad case of cramps or something." Phillip didn't say whether or not he stopped to offer help.

Tim was fast and, as you might guess, went all out in track competition. He set several East Carter track records in the 220 and 440-yard dash, plus the mile relay. He also did well in the triple jump and long jump.

"Track was my sport. It's just you competing against the world. I played some basketball but really didn't like it that much," Tim said.

Fun. Adventure. Even a little danger. Always pushing the limits and, in some respects, living the life of a young and happy Daniel Boone. If ever anybody lived a full life before he left his teen years, it had to be Tim Farmer. But he was getting to the stage where he wanted to move on to something outside his Carter County boundaries. He felt the itch to go where they needed just *a few good men.*

10

Marines

At age 18, Tim was going through a bad case of independence fever. He began to have lots of disagreements with his father over making his own choices. They were typical generation gap conflicts, a common malady, but still uncomfortable for all concerned.

"It wasn't Dad, it was me," admitted Tim.

Tim decided to join the Marine Corps against the wishes of his father and mother. In the discussion with the Marine recruiter about his specific training program, Tim couldn't seem to agree with him, either. Citing good test scores and high general aptitude, the recruiter tried to steer Tim into a highly skilled technical program like air traffic control. Tim had only one thing in mind, however–lots of action.

"I told him I wanted to be in the infantry, that I wanted to go places and fight," Tim said. "I wanted to do what Marines do."

Tim finally agreed, however, to sign on with the Marines as an aeronautics technician and his journey would start in Ashland, Kentucky. His family and girlfriend were standing beside him to wish him well.

"I remember getting on the bus at Ashland...excited," he said. "We drove all the way to Beckley, West Virginia. There were all kinds of recruits at Beckley, male and female. That was where we raised our right hand and were sworn in...It was kind of a sobering moment, really. There was no turning back now."

Having made their promise, the recruits boarded the bus again. They were headed first for North Carolina—and ultimately to the *Marine Corps Recruit Depot at Parris Island*, in South Carolina. Parris Island is commonly known as the toughest boot camp in the Marine Corps. Later, after going through 13 weeks of military hard medicine, Tim Farmer would whole-heartily agree with that presumption. He had always wanted no less a challenge, however.

"We stayed at a place away from Parris Island for a while," Tim recounted. "I think they were waiting for it to get dark so we would get to the place late. Everybody on the bus was loud and excited when we first got going, but as we got closer, people started getting real quiet and the bus started moving slower and slower. Then it stopped. We wondered what was going on. I think they were playing mind games with us."

In a short while, Tim *knew* they were playing mind games, trying to break the green recruits down mentally. "Then we saw this compound in front of us. It had a high gate with barbed wire. Everyone got real quiet and we sat there...and we sat there...Then the gate opened and a bunch of guys came out and started yelling and cursing at us. It was old school Marines there that night. Their aim was to break us down, then build us back up like *they* wanted us."

Tim's cache of Marine memories is huge, even though his stay turned out shorter than he planned. He remembers buddies like "Easter," six-feet, eight inches tall and extremely slow-moving. Easter had a rough time in boot camp.

"The best way to keep your drill instructors off your back was to do things efficiently and as quickly as possible,"

Tim said. Easter did neither. "They were always on poor Easter."

Tim, like his buddies, was very fearful of getting "recycled," or moved back to repeat training, a measure often taken because of an injury or simply a lack of progress. "We were on a march and I had a problem with something in my boot. An object somehow got under my toe and caused a lot of bleeding. We were all so scared to death about getting recycled. I was, too, but as bad as it was, I still just toughed it out."

Rifle training was easy for Tim because of natural ability and his youthful experiences in the woods. The Marines were so impressed with his performance they even talked to him about becoming a range instructor. "That was something I wouldn't even think about. To stay at one place and do one thing was just too boring," he said.

Boot camp at Parris Island was extremely tough, but Tim is totally sold on how the ways of Marine training prepares one for battle. He talked about the respect he developed for his rifle, compliments of Marine protocol.

"Some things you might think were kind of goofy. They had you 'pray to your rifle' each night. But memorizing little phrases like that could help save your life in combat. Marine training helped you to think fast and built confidence. After a while, things started to 'jell' with all the training, and that's when the Marines began allowing you more individual freedom. Things like wearing your uniform a little differently and allowing you to wear your hair with a little more style."

Jonathan Farmer is sure his brother could have been "a good Marine, an exceptional Marine" had he been allowed to stay and make it a career. "The Marine Corps thrives on people with adrenalin and that is what drives Tim today. I know he would have stayed 20 years and then retired."

Deborah, his sister, saw a big change in Tim after his relatively short stint in the military. "Before he left for the Marines, Tim was the type of kid who would take a shower before mowing the yard, then mow the yard with one hand in his pocket. *Cool.* He was always trying to appear cool. Then he'd take another shower after mowing. He was just totally into himself and being *cool.* When he came back from his training, though, he had completely changed. The immaturity had left. He had grown into a man," she said.

11

Great-Granny

They say that if it's in the pedigree, the likenesses will show up somewhere. It just might be true because it worked in the Great-Granny Carr line with respect to great-grandson Timothy Farmer.

To hear Sherry Farmer tell it, her grandmother was a true person of the great outdoors. "Granny Carr was like Annie Oakley when it came to shooting her gun," Sherry said. "You only heard one shot when she hunted for game. That's all it took–one shot. She loved being in the woods shooting game and she loved to fish. And, she dressed just like a man would, too."

Sherry, who stayed with her grandmother and grandfather Carr during a portion of her youth, remembers the night she was laying in bed and heard someone getting a gun ready to shoot.

"I didn't know what to think about it," she said, "I heard the door swing open like someone was walking outside. Then I heard a shot. The next morning, Granny told us that she had to kill a mink that was after her chickens in the coop."

Sherry and her sister often sat on a nearby hill waiting for Granny to return from the woods with her quota of squirrels, something her grandmother did even into her seventies. "She was still living and active when Tim was real little, but he never did really know her. It's just so funny how those two are so much alike in the way they love hunting and fishing." The similarities between grandmother and grandson are uncanny. "Granny just didn't talk about things, she was a doer," said Sherry. "When she was out fishing, she had an intuitive way about knowing what baits to use for particular fish, where to find them, how deep to fish. She found wild greens to eat and for medicinal use in the woods. She was a crack shot. I really believe these traits were passed along to Tim in the gene pool."

Besides the love of hunting and fishing, Granny Carr also adored her flowers. "She didn't always have a lot of money, but every year she would save and send for particular flower seeds out of a catalog," said Sherry. "She had some of the prettiest flower beds you ever saw. Daddy said she had such a green thumb that she could put a broomstick into the ground and it would grow."

Tim's great-grandmother lived an engaging life, dying at age 83. She would have been real proud of her great-grandson, who has kept her reverence for the woods staunchly in the family lineage.

116

12

Parents

When you take a ride with Tim Farmer in his pick-up truck, you first may have to move some things around to create room to sit. Fishing poles, assorted papers, articles of clothing and a pop bottle or two are likely to be in your way. Not unusual for a busy, outdoor kind of a guy, right? What you'd expect... However, when you go into Tim's house, you'll see a neat, tidy and homey place, attractive taxidermy and all. And before you enter his place, you might even feel obliged to take your shoes off, because Tim does.

Tim lives in a world of muddy fields, sticker bushes, the smell of fish and fishing worms, a hectic schedule that can change on a minute's notice and a need to go where the action is. Accordingly, a nice, neat, orderly environment to start and end his day is important to his sense of equilibrium. It might even be a true Godsend. It helps keep Tim grounded. It's a balm for the weary, a security thing.

In reality, though, the refreshing sense of home

most likely came from Sherry, his mother. And that thing about taking the shoes off? Well, it surely came from Mom, too.

Tim learned at an early age that a trek through the woods was fine by Mom, but when he came home, there would be no fussin' about dragging mud into the house. Tim was simply asked to take his shoes off before he walked through the house. He found that the system worked well—and he has adopted it for his own life today in rural Franklin County, Kentucky.

You will find other influences from Sherry Farmer, too. A creative bent, for example. Sherry's finest artistry is expressed through her writing, especially poetry. Quiet by nature, she speaks quite profoundly with written words, as in her poem, *The Woodsman*. Speaking of Tim, she expressed: *"His words are akin to the waters of a wooded stream–rippled waves of sound woven with song..."* Some of her work has been published and one of her deep joys is being a part of a local writing group.

Tim's creative impulses often focus on music, but he has dabbled in visual art, too. He also produces some of the *Kentucky Afield* segments and has added numerous special touches to the programming. The two have appeared several times together, once with fishing guide Randell Gibson on a fishing trip to catch a big striper–which Sherry did–and on a few occasions when she was the subject of Mother's Day adoration by her sentimental son. Viewers were treated to a sampling of her lyrical poetry on those segments.

The Mom and Tim fishing times on *Kentucky Afield* were special, but it took a long time for it to happen. "Mom never had much time to go out fishing when I was little," said Tim. "She had three kids to take care of, a house to clean and she always had meals on the table for us."

But don't think that Mom was so hooked into routine that she couldn't be fun, too. "Mom was the adventurous one," said Tim, "and she would tell stories. They were usually about animals, things like a huge grasshopper and riding on its back. You could tell she was making them up as she went along, but they were great. Mom also would encourage me to draw things and to play certain music. Mom inspired a lot of originality and creativity in me."

Where Mom was incurably spontaneous, Dad showed a strong propensity for order and meticulous planning. "As for being spontaneous, Dad had his moments," said Tim. "He would tell a joke sometimes. He was like Mom as an encourager, though. He was positive to be around. He taught me how to fly fish and started me on the guitar."

Tim said that they both were good to talk to about problems, and neither were prone to be pushy. "For emotional kinds of things, I went to Mom. When I needed to find out what to do or how to do things, I talked with Dad."

Tim noted the sensitivity his father has always had with those around him. "I think that was the reason Dad had his heart attack. He was always so worried about hurting people's feelings."

Commenting on his father as a preacher, Tim said "When he speaks, he is very earnest, very sincere. He always taught us not to be boastful. He is the king of humility. There is not another person like him on the face of the earth."

On a recent *Kentucky Afield* segment, Tim gave tribute to Jerry Farmer in a special Father's Day piece. The two reflected on his father's 40-year-old fly rod that Tim learned how to use in his childhood. After the program, Tim presented Jerry with a brand new fly rod. You can rest assured, however, that the old rod will stay poised and ready to do battle with spirited bluegills, bass and trout in the future.

Sherry talked about a core value that is shared by her husband. "Jerry and I have always been ones who take the side of the underdog. We hope that we have passed that on to our children, and I think we have," she said.

Sherry and Jerry's humble spirit, evident almost immediately to those who meet them, has been passed on to Tim. Though the nature of his job as show host means being "out in front," it's not a way he has orchestrated to massage his ego. The presence of Mom and Dad's decency and grace hovers like a cloud around him. That fact alone won't allow Tim to get too big for his britches.

13

Daughters

If you have been a regular viewer of *Kentucky Afield* over the last decade, you may remember seeing a couple of giggling young girls who showed up periodically. They were either looking for mushrooms, riding in a boat, or maybe doing a little fishing. The two may have seemed a little nervous, plus they may have bore some resemblance to Tim Farmer.

Tim's two daughters, Elizabeth and Rebekah, are similar in appearance. Each has dark, medium-length hair and each has a slender build. By their looks, no one will question the fact that they are sisters. They share some common interests, too. Their personalities are very different, however.

Elizabeth is the reserved one who thinks carefully about her words before she speaks. She might even appear shy at times. But Elizabeth, born in 1986 and recently graduated from Western Hills High School in Frankfort, is the proverbial individual who "knows what she wants." She will be attending Murray State

University in the west end of the state, five hours from home. She will major in music education and plans to teach in high school.

"Some of our youth directors at church went there and they recommended the school," said Elizabeth. "I visited there and it was so people friendly."

Elizabeth, like her father, has a passion for playing music. On the day of her graduation in early June, she was found "jamming" with Tim in his garage, she on the keyboard and he on the drums. This after she had already sung in a group for the ceremony that afternoon. Watching the two, there was an obvious synergy in the sounds they produced and their interaction with each other. Quiet natured Elizabeth and outgoing Dad blended into one.

"Dad used to stay up really late at night and sing and play the piano," she said. He'd have us singing and harmonizing with him. It was a lot of fun."

What's the biggest thing Dad has passed down to Elizabeth?

"Probably his sense of humor. I love to play pranks on people. He hasn't taught me any specific ones, but when I'm playing mine I think he would probably have the same idea." Elizabeth sees some other good qualities in her father. "I think it's great how outgoing he is. I haven't ever seen anything that stops him from doing what he wants. His arm didn't stop him from doing a thing. He always wanted to be in a band, for example, and he made it happen," she said.

Speaking of making it happen, Elizabeth is on a path to make things happen herself. She is currently working two jobs, one as a babysitter and the other at a bakery café in Frankfort. Elizabeth has had a paying job since she was a freshman. "I make payments on my car (bought from a high school teacher) and my cell phone," she said proudly. No one can ever accuse Elizabeth Farmer of taking the easy way out.

Younger sister Rebekah, born in 1987, talks freely on

nearly any subject. She is not reserved like her sister, and rather than be on a track to meet a specific goal, she is still looking incessantly at possibilities.

At the graduation get-together for Elizabeth, in the midst of grandparents Jerry and Sherry, Uncle Jonathan and her sister, Rebekah got the notion to take a spin on the riding lawn mower. She plopped herself on the seat, looked at the different mechanisms and finally figured out how to start the machine. Soon she was 50 yards away on the edge of the large yard, soaking in the warm air, the smells of the nearby woodland, the excitement of trying something novel. The familial spectators paused to see what she would do when the mower quit moving, though the engine continued to roar. Rebekah gave a quick, sideward glance their way, dismounted the seat and looked for the problem. Satisfied, she jumped back on, changed the direction of the wheels, hit the gas pedal hard and finally was on her way, grinning.

Sound familiar? Any similarity to an adventure-loving guy who overcame a huge life challenge to become the dynamic host of America's longest running outdoors show?

Speaking of the "outdoors life," fishing and hunting, Rebekah spared no exuberance. "I love it all. I just don't have time! I work at the bread store, too. I've been turkey hunting with a gun twice, came up short both times. Long story. Been fishing countless times. I've been dove hunting. I actually shot three doves, only found two. I think some little kid stole my other one."

Her dream is to go saltwater fishing, something her father has promised her. "I love the ocean and I'd love to catch HUGE fish. I bet it is such a thrill!"

How does Rebekah compare herself to Dad?

"We are a lot alike. We both love hunting. We have a lot of the same sense of humor and I think we look alike, too. I'm just 'quirky.' That's what my mom calls me. I just get restless. If there's something to do, I'm going to do it," she said.

Rebekah even hints at being a little bit political. "I'm all for NRA (National Rifle Association), but I do think they should check on people's backgrounds."

Rebekah's thoughts on a career? "I'd love to be a runway model. I'd love to be on the catwalk with all the beautiful people. That may seem shallow but...I would also love to design clothes. I wouldn't mind being a singer, too."

Tim weighed in on the conversation concerning his daughters.

"They're as different as night and day. Elizabeth and I have the same taste in music. Rebekah likes the new stuff. Elizabeth is well grounded, Rebekah is spastic like me," he laughed.

Tim is proud of having two girls who are willing to work for things they want. He sees it as a character building way of doing things, a way of learning independence, confidence, and an appreciation for the things obtained.

"My parents gave me that same opportunity, to not be given everything, and I just think that helps young people grow," he said.

Tim and Cheryl, now no longer together, have done a good job raising two solid daughters who seem on their way to a bright future.

14

Memorables

In most of our lives, specific people tend to show up in our thoughts more than others–for good reasons. These folks are memorable in significant, positive ways, not easy to forget. Their stamp has been imprinted indelibly on our minds and hearts because they have changed our lives, or, at least, have caused us to take pause and notice something meaningful. The "specialness" might be the things they say or the way they talk, the way they act or react, the way they treat you, the nugget of wisdom they impart or the bit of humor they espouse. Along the way, Tim Farmer has met some individuals he will always embrace as highly memorable.

Alonzo Gaines

On a 2005 filming segment of *Kentucky Afield,* Tim had as guest Alonzo Gaines of Lawrenceburg, in Anderson County. The topic for the segment centered around finding "wild greens" in the woods and along the roadside. On this day, Tim and viewers got a lot more than a few tidbits on how to balance their fish and game diets with some wholesome vegetation.

The heavy-set, middle-aged African-American man stood waiting for Tim in front of the courthouse on Main Street. Smiling broadly, Alonzo right away talked about being dressed for the occasion.

"I wore my boots for getting' greens. It's tick season and…"

"I like ticks. They're good to eat," kidded Tim as he pulled his Ford pickup out onto the bustling street, watching for a station selling diesel fuel.

"Yeaaaa," Alonzo guffawed loudly with a voice that started deep inside him.

"What kind of greens we looking for, Alonzo?" said Tim.

"Well, now, right now a lot of greens have gone to seed, sorry to say. We'll probably see a lot of yellow mustard. We got polks comin' up real good, too. I got some wild lettuce and I saw some crow's foot the other day…my sister blanches them for 'bout 20 minutes and everything like that."

"What do you mean 'blanching'?" Tim followed.

"Just put 'em in a little water and let 'em boil down and everything like that…A BIG COOKER LIKE YOURSELF AND YOU DON"T KNOW WHAT BLANCHING MEANS?" Alonzo roared, having loads of fun with his escort.

"I cook meat," the escort said. "That's why we got you, to show us how to cook greens. I need some more fiber in my diet."

"You're half way there, ha ha," said Alonzo. "One thing about these greens, THEY WILL CLEAN YOUR SYSTEM OUT."

The bantering kept flowing on the way to Wildcat Road, where the search for roadside salad would take place. The two talked easily about both their favorite game to hunt (squirrels) and how the population of quails was hurt by an ice storm in the late seventies. Encountering poisonous snakes and fishing for white buffaloes and perch was duly discussed. The two men talked with a joy and a healthy, knowing appreciation of nature and its creatures.

"Alonzo, what are we going to do today?" asked Tim as he turned left down Wildcat Road.

"Well, today, we gonna git us some wild greens and HAVE A WILD GREEN DINNER," he answered, and one felt compelled to be as excited as Alonzo was.

They continued riding on the narrowing, curvy road. Tim waited for a sighting of greens from Alonzo. Alonzo looked, but also filled the time with an assortment of his impersonations. He did John Wayne, Cary Grant, Red Foxx, Mr. T and singer Andy Williams singing *Moon River*. After each rendition, both laughed like two kids goofing off, having fun. All this, and the greens were coming, too.

"I just saw some wild lettuce over there," said Alonzo, pointing.

Tim carefully pulled on to the side of the road and the two got out, cameraman Brian following. They walked directly to the wild lettuce.

"Be sure and take the top leaves off...the soft ones, small and tender. If you see something black movin, it's only a snake."

"You afraid of snakes, Alonzo?"

"Naa, I grew up in the outdoors and everything like that."

During the course of the still, sunny morning, Alonzo talked about his work in the church and with the Christian men's group, *Promise Keepers*. He raved about his happy childhood when he hunted, fished, went to local carnivals, and gathered greens. He remarked about creatures he heard in the woods while he looked for greens. Then he mentioned matter-of-factly, "I've learned to listen real good since I can't read and everything like that."

"Alonzo, I hear you know a lot of Bible verses," Tim

prodded.

"Faith comes from hearin' and hearin' comes from the Word of God," Alonzo said. "I learned to listen *real* well." Then he laughed again.

Alonzo kept talking as he harvested wild lettuce, "shiny," lamb's quarters, polk and black mustard. He patiently gave Tim (and the TV audience) tips on how to pick each, assess the ripeness of each plant and where each plant might likely be found.

"Some of these people told me they thought I was the smartest man in the world. They couldn't believe I can't read and everything like that. Just like Tim Farmer, people just can't believe what that man can do." Then he laughed some more.

Because of the greens hunting expedition that morning on Wildcat Road, people were both informed and entertained. But most importantly, some might well have been prodded to find some joy in the little things they encounter everyday.

Larry Thompson

One of Tim's most memorable friends in high school was, he said, "almost anti-hunting. He didn't care about that stuff at all." Larry Thompson, the individual who visited Tim in the hospital and accidentally jarred the bed, causing his friend unbelievable pain, came to Grayson in the ninth grade from Middletown, Ohio. He was a product of a broken home, an individual Tim called "so out of sorts. Everybody thought he was different."

In Tim's mind, Larry had a huge redeeming quality. "Larry had a very high IQ, was a real smart guy, but Larry wouldn't back down from a fight. There was this guy who was in the Golden Gloves who just liked to fight. Larry was walking home one day and the guy made fun of him," explained Tim.

Tim saw Larry shortly afterwards. "Larry was beaten to a pulp. His hair was pulled out and his face swollen. I asked him what happened and he told me about standing up to the Golden Gloves guy," said Tim.

Shortly afterwards, another bully picked a fight with Larry. Again, he didn't back down. Unfortunately, the results were no different from the first time–but he had won Tim's respect. "You had to respect the guy a lot," said Tim. "So I made an effort to befriend him. I was afraid somebody was going to kill him."

Despite some different interests, they grew close. "Larry didn't understand the concept of fishing. He was bored with it. Once we were out in a canoe and I was trying to fish. Larry kept talking to himself and making funny noises." Tim devised a plan to remedy the situation. "I told Larry we needed to go to shore because I had to use the bathroom. When we got off the water, I ran off from him and fished by myself. I left him alone for a long time."

Tim had other memorable adventures with Larry, such as skipping school. One time they skipped, however, was for "educational reasons." They went to the airport at Huntington to see President Carter's arrival. Often, though, they would see movies and "get into all kinds of trouble," as Tim called it.

"One day, I said to Larry, 'Let's go to the recruiting office'." Tim was talking about the *Army* recruiting office in Huntington. It started out as a joke.

"We both spent a lot of time talking to them. We left, then we just died laughing. We weren't serious about it at the time. But guess what? Larry ended up joining," Tim said. "He went to the National Guard and learned how to fly helicopters."

Returning from boot camp, Larry was a changed individual, according to Tim. "He came back all 'locked and cocked' and wouldn't look you in the eye. He looked different and acted different. He cracked me up. I laughed at him until he loosened up again."

Seems like Larry has turned out all right, even with all

the fights gone bad and a bunch of boring fishing trips with Tim. Maybe Tim has played his part in helping Larry get it all together.

Burley and Lardo

Two middle-aged guys were floating down the Kentucky River along the Palisades on a shanty boat. To pass the time, they did some banjo and guitar picking, played on a harmonica, enjoyed a little fishing, engaged in occasional napping–and they cracked a lot of one-liners for whomever might be listening. Mostly, they just had fun. On this bright spring day, Tim and the *Kentucky Afield* production crew were taking advantage of Lardo and Burley's nautical hospitality on a moving tour of their houseboat.

Lardo explained how the trip was to commence. "We've got to get it away from the limbs pretty quick or it'll tear our stove pipe off," he said.

The construction of the shanty by Lardo took a few months. "I told Burley when I first got it done that it's all mine and hand-made. He said it looked to me like you made it with your feet."

The visitors were shown two beds, a table and a heating stove. Then Lardo opened the door of the little room in the middle of the boat. "And we've got all the modern conveniences...an indoor outhouse here..."

He gracefully lifted what looked like a trap door on the floor, explaining that the opening provided a way to "fish in the wintertime." As he did so, a tree branch hanging on the underside appeared, at first glance appearing to be a snake.

Burley screamed and jumped away, then denied he was afraid of snakes.

Tim saw the fishing rods on the craft and asked about them. Pretty soon their lines were wet and someone caught a channel cat. It gave Lardo another opportunity to yack. "I caught an 80-pounder the other day," he said. "For bait I used a baby rabbit and I put the hook on the nape of the neck." Then Lardo looked into the camera told the audience he was "just kidding…"

Tim was chided about "having it made, with his good government job allowing him to go fishing."

Lardo talked about the good life. "There's something about the smell of coffee perking and coal oil lamps burning and listening to *The Grand Old Opry* on a Saturday night. It reminds me of when I was a kid again."

Actually, Lardo and Burley, known as *The Moron Brothers*, are performers who appear regularly at the Renfro Valley in Mt. Vernon, Kentucky. There, they play music and engage in cornpone humor. Lardo's real name is Mike Carr. Burley is actually Mike Hammond. Their web site address is *themoronbrothers.com*

Tim Farmer said the two "defy description" and have made this segment on *Kentucky Afield* "one of the better ones."

Billy Mitchell

Billy Mitchell has a friend for life in Tim Farmer. No matter all the barbs that Billy sends Tim's way. No matter the good-natured inter-department competition that has found them sparring against each other. No matter that "Billy Bob," as Tim calls him, is a "short little guy" and Tim is tall. Billy, as mentioned in an earlier part of the book, was the person most instrumental in putting Tim on the road to archery competency, and that fact will always be remembered by the host of *Kentucky Afield.* A story is told about the time the two traveled together to a conference at a Kentucky state park. While there, they practiced their bow shooting. One of the two missed the target and the arrow broke through a cottage window. Fortunately, no people were in the small building at that moment. The guilty bow shooter made his way into the cottage and retrieved the arrow. That person will not be identified in this book, but each of the two involved know who it is.

Billy Jarboe

What do you say about a six-feet, five-inch tall guy who lost an eye in the Viet Nam War, threw his artificial eyeball toward a doctor after an optical examination, was struck by a Volkswagon, then walked out of a Veterans Administration Hospital while being treated for that car accident?

You might say that Billy Jarboe is a fishing partner and friend of Tim Farmer, that he is a fishing guide on the Green River and he has gone after muskies and walleyes on a couple of *Kentucky Afield* episodes. Plus, you might say that Billy is a very interesting person to be around, wouldn't you?

Billy related that he hit it off real well with Tim starting about six or seven years ago, and now calls him "a role model's role model" for the way he conducts his daily activities.

"Tim just amazes me how well he does things with just one arm. He doesn't get down about it, and since I know what it's like to deal with a disability, that says a lot about him."

Billy laughs a lot, too, especially when Tim and him are in the fishing boat. "Tim does impressions of Elvis, evangelists and kids on that *South Park* show. One time I was down in the bottom of the boat, laughing so hard I couldn't catch my breath."

One thing is for sure. You'll find the two together again, probably many times. They'll fish and laugh and Tim will wait around for something else interesting to happen in regard to Billy Jarboe's life.

Dexter Wilburn

Picture a skinny kid in his early twenties living near you in a small Kentucky town. You've never really met him, but the kid fascinates you. He's out everyday, with all senses alert: *watching, listening, even smelling–and always searching.* He has an air rifle that he uses to shoot small birds in your neighborhood. That is a bit unusual, because air rifles mostly tend to be in the realm of young adolescents. But the most unusual thing about the kid is that he uses only his left arm, often with the gun propped against something stationary. Strangely, his right arm just hangs there, not used. Seems it just goes along for the ride.

Dexter Wilburn, late sixties, sits on his front porch and watches, even studies, the solitary show performance–day after day, shot after shot, bird after bird. The retired coal miner probably discerns a little bit of himself in the kid's movements, that of someone slowly, stealthfully on the hunt for wild game, patiently making himself alert to his prey's habits. And though he sees the passion of the kid, a passion he has himself, he sees that the kid is, in fact, very green.

One day, the senior and the junior's paths cross and they engage in knowing conversation. Dexter talks about "Julie," his prized hunting dog. Dexter and his canine beast have had a wealth of hunting adventures. The young man, Tim Farmer, talks of his Marine Corps stint, his accident and his recent marriage. Though trying not to belittle Boy Hunter, Dexter gently explains that shooting game inside the city limits just might cause more trouble than it's worth. The thought really hadn't occurred to Boy Hunter.

Then Dexter invites Tim to come along with him to the woods, where together they can run the dogs for squirrels and coons. Tim, always looking for adventure of the outdoors kind, is flat out excited. Now the fun has really begun. They hunt, they talk, they share. Dexter is good for Tim. He always brags on him, remarking how he likes the way Tim hunts. He builds him up at a time when Tim has developed some doubts about himself after suffering the motorcycle accident.

The relationship has continued for more than 20 years. Dexter, now in his eighties and in failing health, is no longer able to walk the woods with Tim. Besides that, Tim is quite busy with hosting an outdoors TV program. But Tim will often check in with ol' Dexter when he visits Grayson. They talk of old times and the good hunting dog that Dexter sold to

Tim for $75. Sometimes they just sit there together, soaking in small town life and not talking a whole lot. Besides, they know that each other has hunting on their minds, and that's just as good as conversing, it seems.

15

Celebrities

Tim has discovered that his interest in the outdoor life is shared with a number of celebrities. He has used that fact to add spice to a number of *Kentucky Afield* episodes.

Among those well known are Western Kentuckian Don Everly of the Everly Brothers, a singing duo that gained national prominence in the late fifties and early sixties. Tim found himself crooning along with Don on an episode of *Kentucky Afield* and even appeared at a concert with him. The fact is, one might find Tim using some of the Everly Brothers' material wherever he might go on stage.

The Kentucky basketball world is also covered. Former University of Louisville basketball coach Denny Crum, a person Tim pegs "a good guy and a 'by gosh hard-core fisherman'" did a show with Tim on the Ohio River. Another Farmer, former University of Kentucky basketball player and all-time high school icon Richie Farmer, appeared with his two young boys in a fishing trip to a farm pond. Jeff Shepherd, a two-time member of UK basketball national championships, appeared in a segment fishing at a farm pond and talked about his game warden father.

Tim found that enthusiasm for the outdoors is not exclusive to men. He enjoyed hunting trips with the singing Mandrell Sisters (Irlene got her first turkey on the show).

Another musician, Kentuckian Troy Gentry of the country music duo *Montgomery Gentry,* duck hunted with Tim near Mt. Sterling.

In a *Kentucky Afield* segment filmed in Michigan, rock star Ted Nugent provided a great exhortation to young people–get out in the great outdoors and participate in hunting and fishing and it'll keep you out of trouble! Tim described Nugent as having "a genuine adventurous spirit who recognizes the importance of growing up in the outdoors. He tries to make that available to today's youth. He is very intelligent and has a great deal of energy. He is also outspoken about the outdoors, which rubs some people the wrong way. He's a good role model for being a rock star."

A regular visitor and personal friend of Tim is Byron Crawford, Louisville *Courier-Journal* Kentucky life columnist. His folksy manner and love of fishing are perfect matches for the *Kentucky Afield* program. "Byron and I have a lot of the same interests," said Tim. "We both like old stuff and we've dug around in antique stores together." Their conversations on the show smacks of old-time rural Kentucky culture.

In a 1998 episode, Tim was surrounded by celebrities at a skeet shooting fund-raiser hosted by Irlene Mandrell. On hand were the Hager twins, Jim and Jon, formerly entertainers on the *Hee-Haw* series. Also appearing on the show were Thyme Lewis of daytime soap *Days of Our Lives* along with Ken Hanes of *The Bold and Beautiful.* Former NFL pro Dave Butz and Buck McNeeley of *The Outdoorsman* also participated. *Wind Beneath My Wings* song writer Larry Henley added to the entertainment variety of the show. Tim's relaxed jocularity with the celebrities made it highly watchable and fun. But on a weekly basis, the show is enhanced by Tim's easy sociability with any guest, whether well known or unknown.

16

Angler

During an agonizing time of civil wars in the 1600's, English writer Izaak Walton crafted a book about fishing technique and the simple, positive message of being in tune with the natural world through the practice of "angling." It was called *The Complete Angler*, or, the *Contemplative Man's Recreation.* The book has become, in part, a political classic, one that was written to protest the tumultuous times and to suggest an alternative way of looking at the world. Most of all, it celebrated fishing–done right.

This book's author thought about Izaak Walton's work after a recent sunny and still afternoon in eastern Mason County. It was while fishing with Tim Farmer on a farm pond near Tim's childhood home–the actual pond where Tim spent untold happy hours doing what was second nature to his young soul.

After Tim had said hello to Carol at the white farmhouse off Olivet Church Road, letting her know that he and a friend would spend some time down at the fishing hole, he nosed his diesel-powered pick-up down the hillside to the heavy iron gate. After a quick glance at Tim, the author zipped from the cab, unhooked the small chain from the post and managed, with a bit of difficulty, to open the swinging gate enough to allow for passage. A second opening, this time down the hill, close to the pond, and consisting of two live electric wires, drew a warning from Tim.

"Hold on to the orange handles," Tim said, and the author got the message so that there was no discomforting incident.

The expert and the novice, now both in the truck, crept along the long, level bank on grass trimmed by about a dozen cattle. The expert peered at the quiet, often muddy patches of water along the shoreline, probing for clues, sensing the environment, losing himself in his scouting expedition.

"See those fish under the tree, Steve. They're guarding their nest. There's a lot of bass on the bank here. Yea, we're gonna catch some fish today. Look, there's a patch…there's another. We've come at a good time, Steve."

The expert was getting wound up and slipping into fishing mode, no turning back. After lifting the smallish, two-seated fishing boat down from the back of the pick-up, Tim and the author shoved the boat onto the small dock, then tilted it down onto the still waters.

The author, prepared to watch and tape record but not fish, clumsily boarded the floating piece of fiberglass and sat down cautiously on the right seat, a little self-conscious. Tim, even with the use of only one arm, was more graceful as he settled onto the left seat with a long but lightweight fly rod in hand. In no time, Tim's floating bug, a "popper," was sent on its way toward the bank, close to the dock.

"See that bass that just hit the bug," the expert offered.

"How do you know it was a bass?"

"The way it hit," Tim answered quickly.

Tim kept the line taut as the hooked small bass angled away from the boat. "*That fish was* hungry, can tell the way he took the hook," said Tim. His eyes never left the action on the pond's surface.

Another cast. A quick hit, but the fish escaped the hook.

"That was an aggressive male, Steve. Let's remember that spot. He's trying to protect his fish eggs."

"Is there any chance you could catch a catfish with that popper?" asked the author, showing his ignorance.

"Not very likely. I have, but…"

"What's the smartest fish, the hardest to catch?"

"Walleye. I don't know about the smartest but it's the hardest to catch."

"What if you wanted to catch larger fish than these bluegills and bass?"

"Probably use a plastic night-crawler or some crank bait. On these small ones, I'd put on a smaller hook if I really wanted to catch everyone of them."

Tim was patient–both with the fish and with the author–and he kept reeling bluegills and bass to the boat.

"Steve, we picked a *good* day to be on the water," Tim gushed as he reeled another bass toward the boat. In the boat, Tim's two bare feet became like hands in subduing the frisky fish. He held the line about two feet from the fish's mouth and lowered it to the boat's floor. Almost in the same motion, both feet covered the fish, except for its mouth area. Then he moved his hand to the fish's mouth and deftly, but carefully, retrieved the hooks. He finished the routine by tossing the fish overboard. It was stunned but not hurt. Then he was ready to catch another fish.

The conversation turned to a side issue–losing things in the water while fishing. Yes, the expert had lost things before: sunglasses, wallet, watches, shoes. The law of averages and Tim's complete focus on the important matter at hand, fishing, would easily account for losing things. Just part of it.

For the author in the boat, it was good to hear that the

expert was human, at least when it came down to non-fishing items. He also heard the expert say that cows who wade into the pond destroyed nests and that he wasn't partial to using worms to fish ("you always have to change bait"). Tim educated the author on many little things that day.

Then Tim decided to impart to the author some of the sterling education he had received about 30 years ago from his father–the technique of fly-fishing.

"You ready to do some fishin'?" Tim asked.

"I'm not sure." The answer had a lot to do with the fact that the author had not had a real day of fishing since he was a young teenager---and now to embarrass himself in front of, perhaps, Kentucky's premier outdoorsman?

"Here, take the fly rod, Steve. Now…whip the pole straight up, with force. Then hesitate, one-thousand one, one-thousand two…then whip it forward, not with as much force."

The author jerked the pole straight up with just a little force. Immediately, he shot it forward. The line fell straight down, near the boat and 20 feet from its intended target. The popper and its hooks helped create the beginning of a serious line entanglement problem.

Tim hardly changed facial expression. The two worked together, three hands worth, to free the line and prepare for cast #2.

"Whip the pole straight up, hard. Hesitate. Then whip it forward. It's in the wrist. It really is, Steve."

The author did much better on the next cast. And with the expert's steady coaching and encouragement, the novice fly fisherman caught four fish within the next half-hour, and, more importantly, consistently cast within several feet of the watery target. Plus, he was having fun. Kid fun. In truth, Tim Farmer may have made a lifetime convert to fly-fishing.

As the hours sped by on this comfortable May day, with caught bluegill and bass now numbering about thirty, Tim's attention was shifting to the matter of some very large fish swimming near the surface, particularly in the more shallow end of the pond. It was cause for him to stand up and fix his eyes on some intruders, like Captain Hook watching for pirates.

"Look at those grass carp. I've never seen 'em that big before. They must be 30-40 pounds!"

The expert was prepared for action. "I'm going back to shore a minute," Tim said. "Let me get my bow. You hold onto the fly rod, Steve."

On the bank, the expert zipped to his truck and came back with a different piece of gear, something that looked like a cross between hunting and fishing equipment. It was a bow and arrow with a fishing reel secured to the bow, which meant that the "shot" arrow could be retrieved by reeling it in–a little hunting and a little fishing, too.

Tim again boarded the craft, armed with the hybrid bow and an intense look on his partially tanned face. He soon was standing on two slender, but strong legs. This would give him better vision and better body positioning as he pulled on the 40-lb. pressure bow.

One could sense Tim's adrenalin level rising. Even the untrained eye of the author could see the swirling waves and the darkened shadows that revealed large grass carp on the prowl. Generally, several could be seen together, often with bubbles following behind. Though grass carp are not a danger like sharks, the sight of the fishes on patrol can appear ominous.

"My gosh, Steve. Look how big. Now…let's keep it real quiet. They know we're looking for 'em."

"I just saw one with his *fin* out of the water," said the author.

Just then, Tim locked his eyes on a spot 25 feet in front of the boat. He gracefully raised the bow to eye level and grasped the tab with his jaw teeth, nearly in the same motion. With a deep breath and a tightening torso, Tim pulled the arrow almost full shaft length and released the arrow, line attached. Rather than a whistle sound, it produced a note of muffled wind and plopped hard into the muddy water, showing no sign of hitting the carp.

"Missed it," said the expert quietly, with only a small frown observable. "Those fish are hard to see in the daylight. It's a lot easier at night with lights on the water. But we're going to take one out of here today. I can feel it."

The author reeled in the popper on the fly line. It had nearly been forgotten and was trolling behind the moving boat. He noticed a few minor hits on the bait, but ignored them. He wanted no distractions now. The real action was taking place with the archer and the schools of carp.

"If we hit one of those fish, hold on 'cause it'll take us for some kind of a ride around this pond," said Tim.

"Are you serious?"

"Oh, yeah…they can do it."

There were many moments of quietness except for the soft whirr of the motor and a cow bawling a few hundred feet away. Then…

"Look at *that* pod of fish," said Tim.

Within a few moments one could hear the tension of the bow and drawn string, then another swoosh of the projectile and line, but again there was no indication of blood or of a large carp flopping in the water–and, of course, no ride around the pond.

Still confident, Tim reeled in his arrow and line.

"We'll get one," he said.

More quiet. More intense, visual searching of the pond's surface. An abundance of patience and concentration. *Then, another sighting…*

Tim quietly, slowly, readied the weapon. The glint in his eye showed that the stars were in alignment, that this was the time–he would get the carp.

The shot had a different, hollow sound. The line broke immediately and the arrow sunk into the watery grave, halfway to its target. No grass carp, no weapon, no conquest. Then there was a pause...

"That *finishes* our day," said Tim, who came to the pond with one arrow in his quiver. The words of disappointment were not necessary to say, they were written all over his face.

"I just knew we would get one, but I'm out of arrows."

Then the expert and the author loaded the boat on the truck, traveled back up the hill, and went looking for something good to eat.

Even Izaak Walton gets hungry.

17

Hunter

"**K**illing a deer with a bow is a huge challenge. Killing a *buck* with a bow is an even bigger challenge."

So began an elevated time of sharing wisdom from the woods, wisdom gleaned from many years of deer hunting experience, chiseled and honed by listening to hundreds of other experienced deer hunters. And, perhaps most importantly to Tim Farmer, is the pure, unadulterated respect, even awe, that he holds for the graceful prey.

"Some people hunt their whole lives and never kill a deer with a bow. There are too many elements involved. First of all, the deer's sense of smell is so keen. A deer may smell you a half-mile away."

Tim offers some tips and experiences that might help deal with the heightened olfactory attributes of deer. "There are certain things you have to do. You have to keep your scent as neutral as possible. Before a hunt, I hang my clothes out and set my boots out overnight. I spray neutralizing scent on them. I have taken leaves or needles from spice bush, sassafras, cedar and pine, and boiled them down, mixed together. I take the mixture and put in a spray bottle to use on my clothes. Each house has a particular smell, like the bacon you fry, how well people clean, or don't clean, or pets. These smells become a part of your clothing. I've even bathed in baking soda to get rid of the smells found in my house."

Tim hunted and took deer with a gun many times, but the first deer Tim killed with a bow was in 1991. He talked in detail about all the preparation he used to reach that long held goal.

"I finally had gotten to the point with my bow and arrow that I knew exactly what I could do---shoot and hit a spot the size of a baseball at 20 yards while pulling with my teeth. I had a little farm out in Shelby County and I had seen a bunch of deer there. On the farm was an existing deer stand that someone built years ago. Now, I actually had killed a number of deer with a gun and wasn't particularly challenged by that."

The wheels had started turning in his mind and some severe passion was welling up inside the young woodsman.

"I would go to the tree stand at the break of day, carrying an apple and a bottle of water. Some times I would hear deer walking around but couldn't see them. I seldom spooked the deer and I knew where my 20-yard range was."

One might wonder about the significance of the 20 yards.

"I found that if you shoot five yards past that, your arrow starts to drop, you lose accuracy," he said. He held himself to that way of thinking throughout the long-term project to get his deer with a bow. "I saw multitudes of deer from 23-25 yards, but I had the patience...I was not going to blow a shot because of the distance. One day, a deer got within 10 yards and I pulled back my leather tab, ready to get my first...The leather broke and I lost him. I was tore up for days about it...*losing the deer with malfunctioning equipment was tough.*"

Tim knew he would need to make a change in the tab

material. "That was another lesson learned, that leather cracks and will break. I started using a braided nylon, and it was important to me that I let others know why so I could save them the same problem I had," he said.

Tim admits that his personality sometimes is contradictory, at least in the way he approaches certain tasks. He often has trouble organizing himself to get to the barber shop, to take care of paperwork or other routines. His heavy and hectic schedule accounts for much of that difficulty. On the other hand, he can exhibit intense focus with other tasks.

"I can be spastic, all over the place. If I decide I'm going to do a task that I really zero in on, I crack all my energy into it. I can make everybody miserable because I have tunnel vision with it until I accomplish it," he said.

Tim definitely had his tunnel vision working when it came to bagging his first deer with a bow. He continued his patient, methodical quest, and hopeful signs began to appear.

"Every now and then, in the shadows, I would see this rack. This had become *my* deer. It was almost like somebody with a prize-winning garden who had spent the time and the effort to make it special. I bet I saw this guy (the deer) 15 times."

Then came the showdown.

"It was October 29 and it was ridiculously cold, about 19 degrees. I had been out there in the rain and had braved the mosquitoes and those little gnats that fly up your nose. I had done the homework, put in the time. On weekends or whenever I had time off, I was even out there all day long."

As the sun broke through that morning, Tim heard a "grunt" noise.

"He (the buck) was out about 50 yards chasing this doe, back and forth, back and forth. Then, the doe started walking towards me in the deer stand, looking over her shoulder at the buck. She came within 5-8 yards of me, and I *could* have taken her. The buck appeared to be looking at me but actually had his eye on the doe. It seemed like an hour but was probably about three minutes. Finally, the doe moved off and the buck came up to where the doe had been, right in front of me." It was the moment of truth for both Tim and the buck.

"To me, at the time, there was no bigger challenge in the world. He was standing there, I was standing there. I was solid as a rock. This was the moment...I pulled back, about 58 lbs., so far back that I first extended my arrow too far and had to put it back on the bow. Then I pulled back again, and waited...waited, maybe 15 seconds. I aimed at a particular point on the buck and thought about all my shooting training. There was this calm came over me. Then I released the arrow..."

The deer took the arrow, but not without a dramatic reaction. "The deer wheeled upward and jumped five feet, turned around and ran, making crash and bumping sounds," he said, "I heard the arrow clicking, probably because I shot him with a 32-inch long arrow when I should have used about a 26-inch one. Then...there was silence"

Tim might have been tempted to run as fast as he could to retrieve the buck, but his good sense won out over his emotions. "I had heard that if you have a deer down, give it at least a half an hour. The reason is that if you hit it in a bad spot, one that doesn't quickly kill it, the deer can hear you and get up and run a mile away. You may never find it."

Tim sat in the cold for over 30 minutes. He had come this far in the process. He would not mess things up now.

"Being green, I went to my friend Benjy Kinman, who lived in the area. I was all fired up about things and I wanted his advice, but also I wanted some help in dragging the deer out of the woods. So Benjy helped me track the deer. Not far from where I hit the deer, Benjy found a pool of blood. Then, 40 yards over the hill, we found the buck. Benjy patted me on the shoulder and just raved about how big it was. I was out of my mind with excitement. We dressed it, I had a bunch of venison and the trophy is now up on the wall in my living room."

In Tim's mind, he had long last won his badge of honor---something that couldn't be taken from him. He had worked hard and did it the right way. He had shot a deer with a bow, *as a mouth shooter.*

"I understood at that point that hard work had paid off, that if you do your homework and follow the plan, you can be successful. I saw that I could go above and beyond what I had done before."

It was a big boost to his confidence. His peers at Fish and Wildlife heard about his good news and gave congratulations. Plus, there was an article in the Frankfort newspaper written by Dave Baker, editor of *Kentucky Afield* magazine. Not long afterwards, Tim entered archery contests and did well.

Not bad for a guy who only seven years before carried his still connected, but mangled, nearly useless right arm up an embankment looking for someone to help him stay alive.

18

Stories

Much of the joy of working with others is the strong sense of fraternity that often develops, especially when individuals have similar passions. People love to tell stories on Tim Farmer, partly because there's a good chance he's told one on them, partly because he is so engaged with doing interesting things, and partly because, simply, he has gotten to know so many people around the state and even beyond. The stories have been compiled while talking with the people who know Tim best. They have happened at various times in his life. Following are a sampling of the better ones. Likely, more will come in the future. .

Tim Slone, who directs the Information and Education Division at the Kentucky Fish and Wildlife Department, was a fisheries biologist at the time Tim was hired as a fisheries technician in 1989. Slone related the "monkey story."

"We were doing a catfish study on Kincaid Lake, near Falmouth. We were out there, but there were not a lot of other people on the lake. We looked over on the shoreline and saw this black something, and we couldn't tell what it was," Slone said. "We got closer and found that *it was a monkey.* We shot our johnboat to the bank. The way Tim does, he went right up to the monkey. He stuck his hand right up to it. The monkey latched on to his hand, jerked it into his chest, and bared its teeth and gave a big hiss. Tim thought it had him. It finally let go, but the next day we talked to the man who owned the monkey. He had a whole bunch of scratches on his arm because the monkey often gets aggressive. Tim got lucky that he didn't get bitten himself."

Slone told another story of about the same time period, this one somewhat chilling. "We were doing a study on Taylorsville Lake where you block off a section of lake and put out a fish toxicant, which kills the fish. You dip them out of the water, weigh and measure, then extrapolate the findings for the rest of the lake. I was in one boat and Tim was standing in front of it. Doc Williams, an Eastern Kentucky University professor, was standing in front of the other boat."

What was meant as a practical joke engineered by Slone, where both aluminum boats would gently collide, turned out to be more serious.

"Well, Doc's boat had a little metal piece on the steering console that stuck out and when our boat hit that, both boats stopped dead. Doc Williams shot off headfirst one way and Tim Farmer headfirst the other way. Farmer had his eyes closed because of the poison we put in the water. All you could see was Farmer's boots kicking up out of the water. He thought he was swimming up but he was kicking down. Doc, who was in his sixties, had disappeared from sight and all you could see was his hat floating on the water. But finally, Doc Williams popped up and we towed him to shore and we were able to get Farmer back in the boat. Doc never said anything else about it, but Tim rode me about it for years," said Slone.

Shawn Hencye, a friend of Tim Farmer, talked about their trip to Canada to bow hunt for a bear. "We stayed in a bear stand eating granola bars for about 13 hours," said Hencye. "We were about to leave when we finally saw the bear. It moved under us in the stand, then left. In a little while, it came around again. Tim got a good shot at the bear and hit it. But the thing took off, not dead. We weren't sure where it went."

Potentially, the danger involved might have increased. Now the two were dealing with a wounded—and probably very angry—bear. Wounding the bear also angered a French-Canadian hunting guide, who didn't want to contend with an upset bear in the area he worked. Hencye, fortunately, had been filming the hunt and captured the sight of the bear being hit by the arrow.

"We showed the hunting guide the film and he was relieved about it. He knew the bear would soon die," said Hencye. "We searched for the tracks of blood at dawn the next morning and finally found the bear. It was a huge chore getting the head, the fur coat and the meat out of that wilderness We had to walk about 500 yards. The skin and the head weighed over 100 lbs. It looked like we were in some sort of a monster movie."

For the pure fear factor involved, Hencye noted that the hunt for wild boars in Georgia was worse than bears, though the animals are much smaller. "The boars are very unpredictable. We had a boar chase us up onto the back of our trucks. Down below us he just kept popping his jaws, making a loud noise," Hencye said.

"They have trained dogs to track theses pigs down. The pigs do a lot of damage to crops. They're a real problem there. Anyway, they actually put flak jackets on some of the dogs to keep them from getting killed," Tim said.

The boars, themselves, are very hard to kill. "I shot an arrow directly into a boar's neck, which didn't kill it. I then used my .45, then my .380 and it still wasn't completely dead," Tim said. "The meat you get from them is really tasty, though." You'd think a tough boar would produce tough ham.

Not all of Hencye's and Tim's challenges are directly related to the animals they hunt, however. "Shawn and I were driving down a real rough road on a bear hunt, going about 20 miles per hour," said Tim. "Some of our hunting partners had left bear spray, kind of like pepper spray, in our truck. All of a sudden, Shawn gulps, opens the door and rolls out of the truck. Then, the same thing happened to me and I slammed on the brake." Both men experienced nausea, a loss of control and a tremendous amount of mucous flowed from their noses. "Man, we were sick," said Tim.

Hencye explained what caused the messy situation."I thought there were some kind of poisonous toxins coming out of the engine. What happened was that my back pack fell out of the back seat, hit the bear spray can and sprayed it directly under the seat, into the ventilation system. It hit me right in the face. The only thing I could think of was to get out of the truck quick. I got down into a mud puddle to splash my face. I didn't care what was in the water," he said.

Things soon settled a bit, but the ghastly smell lingered. "Everything we ate for a while tasted like pepper spray," Tim said. "You can't believe how much snot is in your body. It was just hanging down to our knees. It reminded me of the Marine Corps gas chamber we had to go through in boot camp."

Award winning nature artist Rick Hill, also a fisheries technician who worked with Tim when he started in 1989, told of the time they were scheduled to electro-fish in a farm pond in Nelson County.

"We were working with the owner to help him make improvements in his game fish management," said Hill. "The man had gone to the trouble to set aside the time in his schedule that morning. We arrived at his place, ready to go, and Tim and I thought each other had loaded the 'shock box,' which you *have* to have to do the electro-fishing. So we came all that distance and couldn't do what we came for. Neither one of us wanted to say anything to the man, but fortunately he was good-natured about it. He let us come back late that afternoon after we handled other appointments."

Hill also related how Tim's playful side can cause unexpected complications. "Tim and I were down in a creek working, and he was skipping some rocks across the water. I told him, 'Tim, you're getting pretty close, you're getting pretty close.' Sure enough, he skipped a rock that hit me in the shin and drew blood. He felt real bad about and apologized over and over," Hill said. "He's a practical joker and he is often very impulsive about things."

Phillip Green, who may know Tim as well as anyone, recalled what appeared to be another chilling episode in Tim's life—another traffic accident, this time while driving a van.

"Tim was driving a van and I was following him in cold weather. He ran into a patch of ice on a bridge and flipped the van over. It hadn't really been that long since the motorcycle accident and I was terrified."

What Phillip didn't know was that Tim, now no stranger to being close to death, gave himself a quick, but thorough, assessment of his injuries, and they were minor. He was a little sore and a piece of glass had made a small cut in his forehead. It didn't look pretty but it was not serious. In what Tim today calls his "jaded" sense of humor, he couldn't resist playing another one on his buddy.

Phillip continued, "There was Tim laying there next to the van, blood on his face and he looked hurt real bad. When I got close, he looked at me, laughed and said something like, 'Hey, this is funny, isn't it?' He was messin' with me. He jumped up and ran away from me. He wasn't really hurt at all."

Sister Deborah weighed in with this short one. "Like I said, Tim and I fought all the time when we were kids and I didn't want him following me around. One time when he was *real little* he followed me over a fence. I got over OK but he got his pants caught and was stuck on the fence. I just left him there. Mom came and got him a little later. They used to say that I 'ruled the roost' when it came to Tim. That's probably true."

Sherry Farmer played along with Tim and his friend Adam when they decided they wanted to play "Superman." "Tim was about seven and we were living at the married housing section at Georgetown College. I found them some towels and tied them into knots, then took crayons and made Superman images. I gave them some parameters about where they could go play, then I let them take off. I found out later that they had gotten up on some of the married housing roofs, which were only about ten feet tall, *and were jumping off.* I think they thought they could fly," she said.

Sherry related another animal story involving Tim. "Jerry was always bringing animals home for the kids. This time, he brought a big bullfrog and we kept it in the bathtub for a day, but I told Jerry we needed to get rid of it. I gathered the troop together, Jonathan, Debbie and ten-year-old Tim. Tim handled the frog and we walked down the road together toward the water. I helped put Tim over the fence and directed him to take the frog down to the pond. There were some hogs grazing in the area and they started coming toward him. I yelled for him to run back up to the fence because the hogs could run pretty fast. I picked him up and swept him over the fence just in time. The hogs were snapping at his heels."

Tim's brother-in-law, Greg Suttles, shared a story related to filming a *Kentucky Afield* segment. "My buddy had bragged on how good his dog was for weeks. So we talked about going hunting with Tim (for the show) for a long time. My buddy finally decided he would. So Tim and his cameraman came and met us. We were going rabbit hunting and my buddy took his dog, Jake. We went off to Greenup County and my buddy let Jake loose. Jake ran off to the woods for a few minutes, then he came back and stood there right with us. We gave him the benefit of the doubt, and we all started walking.

We kicked some brush aside and so forth, but Jake was walking behind us. We probably walked a mile or so and Jake just sat down. He got tired. Then Tim, who had been so patient, told my friend, "I believe I'd get rid of that dog if I were you."

The group, led by the incompetent Jake, had spent all day in the woods. They only shot at two rabbits. The Jake segment was not used for the program, but scenes of the beautiful woodlands of Greenup County were shown instead. Jake has decided to retire from TV work, at least for now.

Jeff Juett and a friend met Tim for a fishing excursion on Lake Cumberland. The temperature was a cold 20 degrees. They met a lightly dressed Tim, who took one look at them and laughed hard, all in good nature. "We had come dressed in about five or six layers, so as not to take any chances with the cold. As it turned out, Tim had a boat with a canopy and a heating stove that provided plenty of warmth. He laughed even more when he watched us take all those layers off," said Juett.

For Tim, anything worth doing is worth doing with fun.

19

Pain

Despite his super active lifestyle, despite his upbeat manner and zest for life, despite what he has accomplished, the truth is that Tim Farmer seldom has a minute that he is without physical pain. And unlike his year of recuperation, when physicians prescribed regular doses of pain medication—leaving him drowsy and somewhat lifeless, Tim seldom takes any medication for the daily discomfort he bears. Besides the distasteful, zombie-like feeling he abhors, Tim remembers the time while in the hospital when he was taken off a certain pain medication.

"I went through withdrawal symptoms and I just thoroughly freaked out," he lamented. It is a truism in his life that he would rather keep himself under his *own* control.

"The pain is always with me," he said matter-of-factly. "Sometimes it is worse than at other times, but it never stops. There's lots of nerve damage. A lot of the pain is stiffness for not being in use."

He has a plate with screws implanted at the level

of his right shoulder because of a loss of bone mass. "The muscle around the plate has atrophied and it causes a lot of stretching of the tissue. At its worst it's like sticking your arm in a deep fryer." The right arm, not surprisingly, is very thin compared to his left.

Will Tim always keep the glove on the right hand? Probably.

"My hand still has some feeling, and it gets real cold, almost freezing. Heat feels good on my hand. The glove helps that and also keeps it from getting banged around, gives it some stability. I actually don't always know where my arm is. More than once, I have shut the car door on it. Also, you know how your feet sometimes go to sleep? The area at the end of my right arm feels that way all the time."

Tim mentioned several things that help with the discomfort. All pretty much fit into the category of distractions rather than relief. Things like listening to his CD's rather loudly as he drives his truck. Warm weather helps, and he talks about moving to Florida some day---where he could also enjoy plenty of salt-water fishing, something he relishes.

Obviously, the outdoors focus as a vocation and a hobby is crucial to handling the daily pain challenge.

"I tell people who have similar disabilities to me to forget the medicine and *be active,* " he said. "Some people get wrapped up too much in the pain. That's hard not to do, but it's important to get your mind on other things."

Sleeping is more than an automatic ritual for Tim, who tries to get six hours per night. "I try to get myself ready to go to sleep immediately when I go to bed, less time to have to deal with the pain." How he positions himself in the bed is very important. "There is *no* comfortable position in bed. There is just *not* one. Some of the times when I have had extreme pain over a long period of time have come when I slept in an odd position on my shoulder and arm."

What keeps your spirits up?

"Doing things I enjoy doing and knowing that there are people a lot worse off than me. I just don't let myself get down. You only go around once in this life, and I want to enjoy it, whether it is the excitement of saltwater fishing or big game in Canada or Africa."

20

Restored

Tim Farmer, 40-years-old, nosed his Ford pick-up out onto I-64 heading eastward to Washington, D.C. It was in July of 2004, and he was going to a place he hadn't gone in a long time—Walter Reed Hospital. Nearly 20 years, to be exact. He had been asked to speak to a group of injured military personnel. The gathering represented most U.S. armed services and nearly all were hurt in Iraq. Many had lost limbs or other debilitating injuries. There were both men and woman in the group, and nearly all were youngish, about 20-years-old.

Driving through mountainous and woodsy West Virginia and Virginia, Tim thought intently about the last two decades of his own life. There was the excitement of joining the Marines and the rigors of basic training, the motorcycle wreck and the extended hospital stay. He pondered the period after he was released from the hospital and military service, a time of serious adjustments, *truly a makeover*, of a life that had been just fine with him until that Sunday afternoon in June of

1984. Seeing the vast, hilly woodlands and smelling its own special brand of perfume, Tim fought back tears as he remembered his first day at Fish and Wildlife. He posed questions to himself. *Am I a lucky man, or what? How can a person get paid for doing what gives his life substance?* Like a tasty piece of cake with extra icing on the top, his decade long stint as host of an outdoors TV show filled him with that "blessed" feeling, much like the one Dad used to talk about in church.

Seeing a place to pull his truck off the freeway, he parked and walked toward a small patch of the great Blue Ridge Mountains. He felt alive as he ambled a few hundred feet into a canopy of green and freshness. For nearly an hour, he meditated on what he would say at Walter Reed. He wanted to express the things that had happened to him these past 20 years. He *must* express, rather, and he *needed* to do it with heart. Far short of relating a step-by-step, how-to clinic to the injured troops, he felt sure that he had some words he could share that might help. As moments passed, Tim allowed himself to drift into a near trance. He pictured the mind-set of a typical troop sitting before him, based credibly on his own experience. The troop was likely scared, though maybe not admittedly. *Fear knocks on the door continually*, Tim thought. He remembered the searing questions bombarding *him* in 1984: *What about this awful physical discomfort? Will it ever diminish, especially without taking this medication? What about me, especially when I get out of this place? How do I look, and what will people think? Will I be able to work a job, and will it be one I really like? What do I need to do---now?*

Dredging up the past was not pleasant. Tim had always preferred to focus on the positive, an attitude that, frankly, had bothered a few people around him periodically. As he thought about what he'd say, though, he wanted every word to be beneficial, hopeful and a plea to take positive control of one's own choices. Never, he surmised, had he wanted to choose his words more carefully. He felt almost a sense of grief as he departed his temporary cathedral and moved back to his truck.

After the extended time of reflection while he traveled, Tim was now approaching his destination. He navigated through snarling traffic inside the metro area of the nation's capital, then made his way to the Walter Reed Hospital parking lot, purposefully plenty early. He was in no hurry, though. This was a time and place he needed to absorb. He needed to see the birthplace of the second half of his life, hear the sounds of a military hospital again, smell the stale smells again…Tim had come a long way. It took him 20 years to get here. He planned on leaving later, when his business was completed, knowing truly what was behind him.

After he had somewhat gotten his bearings, Tim caught up with his contact person, who escorted him to the room where he would make his presentation. In what has to be called a huge irony, *it was the exact room where Tim spent many hours two decades ago.* It was the place where he received his all encompassing advice for living successfully after release from the hospital—*if you can't tie your shoes, go get some kangaroo Velcro shoes from K-Mart.* For these young and vulnerable people facing crises, he hoped he could do better than tell them where to buy their shoes.

Tim patiently began to pull out his props and lay them on a table. That would be his bow, a rifle and assorted other adaptive fishing and hunting gear. He also loaded the DVD player for showing a series of Tim Farmer action clips. As he prepared, individuals quietly began to file in and take a place at one of numerous tables. They were young and washed out in appearance, but mostly they looked scared. *There I was, skinny and pale*, he thought. *That was me. Was I that vulnerable looking?* The passion began to heat up in Tim's spirit, maybe even more than when he shot his first deer with a bow. He would give them his heart and his mind.

The room slowly filled, with maybe as many as 30 finally settling into a bland, floor-matted room used for physical therapy. It got quiet. Tim, tan and dressed casually with shorts, sandals and his long sleeve and glove covering his right arm, gazed intently, but not condescendingly, over a rag-tag crew of injured souls. Physically, mentally, emotionally… all were injured, some worse than others, but all, truly, had obvious afflictions. Tim could see it in their eyes as well as their bodies.

Tim rolled the video. Judging by eyes that widened, the interest level picked up quickly. The audience saw a fully engaged, energetic and playful-looking adult shooting guns and bows, casting fishing line and standing tall on a boat floating in clear, blue water. He looked like a kid who had been turned loose for the first time in Disneyland. What was most clear was that this man used just one arm in all his activities---and he also sported one big smile that wouldn't leave his handsome face. As the video closed, many in the audience were mesmerized and waited anxiously to hear what this speaker had to say.

"I was *you* sitting out there in this room 20 years ago," Tim said. "I know a little about how you're feeling. You're probably wondering about your future, how you look to others…Your body may hurt. You may hurt inside. You have lots of questions, lots of frustration…"

Tim began to demonstrate his adaptive fishing gear, his bow shooting with a tab, the way he used a rifle, and all the little things, and the ways, that help him do what he loves to do. He spoke in a conversational voice, like leaning over the fence and talking to his neighbor. Eyes and ears were pointed squarely on him. Both Tim and his audience were locked in to each other. Then Tim carefully set his props down and shifted his gaze on about 30 kindred souls in front of him. He had more to share with them.

"While I was in the hospital for that year, I used my energy to figure out how I was going to do things that brought me joy. Yea, there were some things I had to let go of, like, partly, my music…but, as you can see by the film and these things

I'm showing you here today, I'm now enjoying my life…A long time ago, when I was sitting down in this room, *just like you are now*, I worried about how I looked, actually a whole lot." Then Tim pulled back the sleeve on his right arm, presenting a bean-pole shaped upper bicep-tricep area that didn't match the left limb at all. Tim could sense the relief by watching their body language. Then he continued. "Today, lots of people watch me every week…people in Kentucky, Illinois, Tennessee and other places. They see someone who sat right where you are now who has fun, someone who has made the world his playground, someone who doesn't feel sorry for himself…but, I want to say to you that it hasn't always been easy. It's taken a lot of work, a lot of determination…"

Tim took a deep breath.

"Maybe you won't take the same track I did. Maybe your interests are different than mine. Maybe you won't ever be on TV…I didn't plan to be on TV when I was at Walter Reed. But, *you have the ability* to decide how you're going to handle what I call, not a handicap, but a simple, daily *aggravation*. I just want to say to you, *be active and find your own playground in this life…*"

Then Tim made himself available to talk individually to each person who expressed a desire. One individual proudly handed Tim his advanced technology prosthetic arm. Another showed an example of high-level plastic surgery on what formerly was a disfigured face. Tim shared a laugh with one who tried eating his food without the use of both of his hands. There were lots of questions about specific adaptations for the things Tim did. It was a good time, with special moments that would rival some of Tim's best.

Tim gathered up his fishing and hunting gear and walked with a bounce out of Walter Reed Hospital that day. He had expended energy he didn't know he had. It was way past the adrenalin stage he usually operated on. He felt that he had helped a few people, suggested a different way to think, gave a little more reason to hope. He felt a little less physical pain that day, a little less of that dreaded coldness in his hand. It was a day he wouldn't forget.

From Walter Reed Hospital, the woodsman would return with a rush to Kentucky...*fully restored.*

An intense moment
of bow fishing.
Photo compliments of
Walt Kloeppel

Kentucky Afield call-
in.
Photo compliments of
Kentucky Department
of Fish and Wildlife
Resources

Happy to be a
Kentuckian.
Photo compliments of
Kentucky Department
of Fish and Wildlife
Resources

Tim imparts "deer wisdom."
Photo compliments of Kentucky
Department of Fish and Wildlife
Resources

Tim examines a trophy deer.
Photo compliments of Kentucky
Department of Fish and Wildlife
Resources

(opposite page) Behind the scenes.
Photo compliments of Kentucky
Department of Fish and Wildlife
Resources

(opposite page top)Tim and the *Kentucky Afield* crew.

(opposite page bottom) Tim, with a little help from his friends.

Retrieving an arrow at archery practice.

(below) Bulls eye!
Photos compliments of Kentucky Department of Fish and Wildlife Resources

Filming the host.
Photo compliments of Kentucky Department of Fish and Wildlife Resources

(opposite page) In a word ... fun!
Photo compliments of Kentucky Department of
Fish and Wildlife Resources

Alonzo Gaines shows
TV viewers prize wild-
flower.
Photo compliments of
Steve Flairty

(below)
Tim and Alonzo
examine the wild-
flower harvest.
Photo compliments of
Steve Flairty

Tim with cameraman Brian Volland on a turkey hunt in Greenup County.
Photo compliments of Steve Flairty

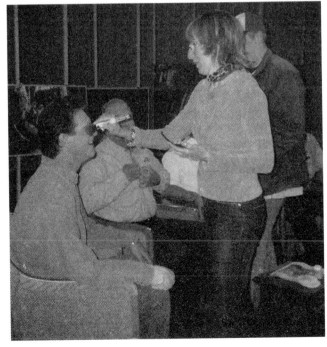

Tim being "made-up" for a *Kentucky Afield* call-in show.
Photo compliments of Steve Flairty

Don't tell your dentist, Tim.
Photo compliments of Kentucky Department of Fish and Wildlife Resources

Appendix I

Recipes

uss "Uncle Russ" Chittenden and Matt Falcone are two connoisseurs of wild game recipes who have made guest appearances with Tim on *Kentucky Afield.* Following are a sampling of Russ's favorites, taken from his two published books, *Uncle Russ's Way (Good Ole Boys Cookbooks, Paducah, KY, 1995)* and *Good Ole Boys Wild Game Cookbook (Image Graphics, Inc., Paducah, KY, 1989).* Having been raised in Cajun Louisiana, Matt is quite familiar with preparing game food. He currently is the chef and owner of *Bayou Bluegrass Catering* at *The Red Mile* race track in Lexington, Kentucky.

Chef Matt offers this advice for diminishing the "wild" taste in game food. "I use a basic solution of water and vinegar. Soak the meat in the refrigerator, covered. Allow 10-24 hours. Put one tablespoon of vinegar per quart of water. It's critical that you don't mix too much vinegar. You can also put sliced, yellow onions in the solution.

The way you process the meat is also important. I hang my game up by the head. If you hang it by the feet, everything in the stomach goes right over the meat. Try to drain all the blood out and don't cut into the organs."

He also extols the virtues of wild game for eating healthier. "The meat tends to be lean, especially rabbit, squirrel and deer. It's pretty organic stuff. No growth hormones and the game are vegetarians. It's a natural product from the start."

A staple of wild game Cajun cooking is the "roux," used for thickening sauces, gravies, and soups and giving a distinctive taste. Matt explains how to create the roux.

"Roux is made from equal parts flour and oil. Add one-half cup of vegetable oil to the skillet. Heat it up so it is almost smoking. Add three-fourths cup of flour, stirring with a wooden spoon on a constant basis. Otherwise, the flour will burn. It will become the consistency of peanut butter, a dark brown, almost black color."

Enjoy. It's all in the "game"!

Recipe Selections from Uncle Russ's Way

Fried Catfish Good Ole Boy Style

Generally served to a crowd, no quantities are shown. However, you can figure that one pound of dressed fish with the "bone in" will be required per person. If fish are selected, a half-pound of boneless fish per person will suffice. One cup of cornmeal will coat about 3 pounds of fish.

Catfish, skinned and cleaned, cut into fairly uniform pieces
   (2"x3"x1") and refrigerated until used
Cornmeal
Salt, 1/2 tsp. per cup of cornmeal
Black pepper, 1/4 tsp. per cup of cornmeal
Cayenne pepper, 1/8 tsp. per cup of cornmeal
Paprika, 1/2 tsp. per cup of cornmeal
Oil (peanut oil, vegetable oil or lard),
   enough for kettle to be 1/2 full

Combine the cornmeal, salt and black pepper, cayenne pepper and paprika in a shallow dish. Dredge the fish pieces in the cornmeal mixture and drop a few pieces at a time into the kettle so the temperature of the oil can be maintained reasonably well. The oil should be kept just under smoking hot..., say 370-380 degrees F. A thermometer partially submerged in the oil will assure this. Cooking time will be roughly 8 to 10 minutes. The fish will be brown and float when it is done. Drain the fish on paper towels before serving.

Serve with hush puppies, slaw and potato salad.

Equally good with bass, crappie, sauger, bluegills...whatever.

Venison Steak-Country Fried

2 lbs. venison steaks about 3/4" thick
1 1/4 cups all purpose flour
1/2 tsp. salt
1/4 tsp. pepper
1/4 cup bacon grease
1 Tbs. garlic juice
1 qt. water
1/2 cup all-purpose flour
1 1/2 tsp. browning and seasoning sauce
1/2 tsp. salt
1/4 tsp. pepper
1 medium onion, thinly sliced
8-oz. can button mushrooms
8-oz. pkg. medium egg noodles, prepared per package directions

Cut the meat into serving-size pieces and beat each piece to
1/2" thick with a meat mallet. Combine the flour with the
1/2 teaspoon salt and 1/4 teaspoon pepper in a shallow dish.
Dredge the steak pieces in the mixture. Heat the bacon grease
in a large skillet. Add the garlic juice and meat and brown on
both sides. Remove from the skillet and set aside.

Add about 1/2 cup of the water in the flour gradually in a
mixing bowl, stirring until smooth. Add the remaining water
and stir. Add the flour mixture to the pan drippings; cook
over medium heat, stirring constantly until thickened. Add
the browning and seasoning sauce, 1/2 teaspoon salt and 1/4
teaspoon pepper and stir. Enough stirring. Return the venison to the skillet; cover, reduce heat and simmer for 30 minutes. Add the onion, cover and simmer for 15 minutes. Add
the mushrooms, cover and simmer an additional 15 minutes.
Serve over the egg noodles.

Serves 6

Duck and Wild Rice

3-4 cups cubed meat, 2 ducks (mallard, gadwall, pintail, etc.),
   skinned and cleaned
3 ribs celery, chunked
1 onion, quartered
1 tsp. salt
1/2 tsp. pepper
6-oz. pkg. seasoned wild and long grain rice
1 stick margarine
1/2 cup chopped onion
1/2 cup flour
8-oz. can mushrooms, drained, reserving juice
1 1/2 cups half-and-half
2 tsp. parsley flakes
1 1/2 tsp. salt
4-oz. pkg. sliced almonds

Combine the duck meat, celery, quartered onion, 1 tsp. salt
and pepper in a stockpot. Boil, in enough water to cover, until
tender or about 1 hour. Remove the meat and cube, being
sure to remove all skin, tendons, etc. Reserve and strain the
broth.

Cook the rice according to the package directions. Melt the
margarine in a skillet. sauté the chopped onion. Stir in the
flour. Add the mushrooms. Add enough of the duck broth
to the reserved mushroom juice in a small bowl to make 2
cups of liquid. Add the liquid to the onion mixture. Add the
half-and-half, parsley flakes and cooked rice and stir well.
Place the meat and rice mixture in a coated 2-quart casserole
dish. Sprinkle with the almonds. Bake, covered, at 350
degrees for 20 minutes. Uncover and bake an additional 10
minutes.

Serves 6

Hasenpfeffer

2 cups dry red wine
1/2 cup 5% vinegar
1 medium onion, sliced and separated into rings
2 bay leaves
6 peppercorns
3 whole cloves
2 1/2 tsp. salt
3 Tbs. brown sugar
4 juniper berries
1 Tbs. dried parsley flakes
2 1/2 lbs. rabbits, skinned and cleaned, cut up
1/4 cups bacon drippings
1 1/2 Tbs. flour per cup of marinade for making gravy
1/2 cup red currant jelly

Combine the wine, vinegar, onion, bay leaves, peppercorns, cloves, salt, brown sugar, juniper berries and parsley in a large plastic bowl. Pour the marinade over the rabbit in a plastic bowl (or something the vinegar won't eat up) and refrigerate for 24 hours. Remove the rabbit, saving the marinade. Dry the rabbit and brown in a skillet in the bacon drippings. Place the rabbit in an ovenproof casserole dish. Remove the onion rings from the marinade and sauté them in the bacon drippings. Add to the rabbit. Strain the marinade, discarding any solids. Measure the marinade and make a paste using the flour. Add the jelly and cook over a medium heat until thickened. Add to rabbit, cover and bake for 1 hour or until tender.

Serves 8

Crock Pot Squirrel

2 squirrels, skinned and cleaned
Salted water
1 medium onion, chopped
1/4 tsp. thyme
1/3 cup bacon, uncooked and minced
4-oz. can button mushrooms, drained
1 cup beef bouillon
1 cup sour cream
2 Tbs. lemon juice
Flour
Fresh parsley

Cut the squirrels into serving-size pieces. Soak overnight in a large bowl, in enough salt water to cover, in the refrigerator. Remove from the refrigerator, drain and pat dry. Place the meat in the crock pot. Add the onion, thyme, bacon, mushrooms and bouillon and stir. Cook for 6-8 hours on low. Remove the meat. Add the sour cream, lemon juice and enough of the flour to thicken. Pour the sauce over the meat, sprinkle with the parsley and serve.

Serves 4

Rabbit could be substituted with equally wonderful results.

Whole Fried Wild Turkey

14-20 lb. wild turkey, cleaned
Old Fugate Dry Mix
5 Tbs. Louisiana hot pepper sauce
16-oz. bottle Italian dressing
6 Tbs. Worcestershire sauce
5 gallons cooking oil

Sprinkle the turkey liberally, inside and out, with the Old
Fugate Dry Mix. Place the turkey in a roaster pan. Combine
the hot pepper sauce, Italian dressing and Worcestershire
sauce in a bowl to make a marinade. Pour the marinade over
the turkey and marinate in the refrigerator for 8-12 hours.
Remove and drain for 30 minutes before frying. Heat the oil
(very hot) in a large deep pot on an outdoor gas burner.
Lower the turkey into the hot oil. Cook 5 minutes per
pound, turning several times.

It's amazing how good this is. The turkey will be juicy on the
inside; crispy on the outside. There are those who, while the
turkey is cooking, quarter a bunch of potatoes, dip them in
the turkey marinade and add them to the pot when the turkey
comes out. They will float when done.

Recipes from Good Ole Boys Wild Game Cookbook

Aluminum Foiled Venison Pot Roast

2-3 lb. venison roast
1 1/4 cups water
1 envelope dry onion soup mix
1/2 tsp. salt
1/2 tsp. black pepper
1/4 tsp. cayenne pepper

Place the roast in the center of a square sheet of heavy-duty aluminum foil. Pour the water over the roast. Add the soup mix, salt and pepper evenly over top of the roast. Bring the edges up to form a pouch or envelope. Pinch together the edges of the aluminum foil to form a tight seal. Place the pouch in a shallow baking dish. Bake for 1 1/2 hours at 325 degrees. Remove the roast to a hot platter and thinly slice. Ladle the gravy over the meat.

Serve with potatoes or noodles as accompaniment.

Serves 4

Dabbling Duck on a Toothpick

Duck breasts (skinned)
Bacon slices
Italian seasoning
Black pepper

Slice the duck breasts across the grain in strips about 1/2"
wide. Wrap with 1/4 of the bacon slices and secure with
toothpicks. Sprinkle with the Italian seasoning and pepper.
Arrange on a baking sheet and broil on the low oven rack
until the bacon is crisp. Drain.

Venison Marinade

1 cup vinegar
1/2 tsp. dried sage
1/2 tsp. thyme
1 tsp. dried mint or 1 Tbs. chopped fresh mint
2 Tbs. minced onion
1 cup vinegar
3 cups olive or vegetable oil

Soak the herbs and onion in the vinegar and oil overnight.

Rabbit in Onion Sauce

2 to 2 1/2 lbs. young rabbit
1/2 cup flour
2 Tbs. salt
1/2 tsp. pepper
6 strips fat bacon, chopped
10 1/2-oz. can undiluted onion soup
1 cup sour cream, warmed
2 quarts water
1 tsp. salt

Cut the rabbit into serving-size pieces. Combine the flour, salt and pepper in a shallow dish. Dredge the meat in the mixture, coating all the pieces.

Fry the bacon in a deep, heavy skillet or Dutch oven until transparent and light brown. Add the meat and brown on all sides. Add the soup, sour cream, water and salt, stir and lower the heat. Cover tightly and simmer for about 1 hour or until the meat is tender, yet not falling from bones. Serve with whipped potatoes and Po' Folks Spiced Cabbage.

Serves 4

Po' Folks Spiced Cabbage

1 firm head white cabbage, about 2 lbs.
6 Tbs. vegetable oil
6 Tbs. white vinegar
4 Tbs. sugar
6 whole cloves
4 large cooking apples, peeled, cored and sliced
1 tsp. salt
4 Tbs. (2 shot glasses) Triple Sec or curaçao

Coarsely shred or thinly slice the cabbage. Heat the oil in a large, deep skillet or Dutch oven. Add the cabbage and stir to throroughly coat with the oil. Add the vinegar, sugar, cloves, apples, salt and liquor and stir. Simmer, covered, for 1 hour over a low heat.

Surprisingly good with goose, venison, duck, cottontail rabbit or spotted guinea pig.

Serves 8

Spiced Carrots

3/4 cup water
3 lbs. carrots, sliced 1/4" thick
1 cup dark seedless raisins
1/2 cup butter or margarine
1/3 cup finely chopped onion
2 tsp. ground cinnamon
1/4 cup packed brown sugar

Combine the water, carrots, raisins, butter, onion and cinnamon in a 4-quart saucepan and stir. Cook, covered, over a low heat until the carrots are fork tender, stirring occasionally...probably 40-45 minutes. Add the brown sugar and cook until the sugar is dissolved. Serve with baked collared peccary, white fronted goose or fillet of Montana widgeon.

Appendix II

Organizations

Much of Tim Farmer's interest has been helping others who have suffered similar physical challenges. He has offered encouragement and practical advice to many, often through the auspices of organizations that specialize in helping people overcome physical disabilities. Tim would heartily recommend your support of the following organizations in Kentucky.

CARDINAL HILL HEALTHCARE SYSTEM
*Cardinal Hill Rehabilitation Hospital, Lexington
Phone 859-254-5701, email
cardinalhill.org/rehabilitation/index.html

*Cardinal Hill of Northern Kentucky, Florence
Phone 859-525-1128, email cardinalhill.org/northern/index.html

*Cardinal Hill Rehabilitation Center/Easter Seals of Louisville
Phone 502-732-5333, email
cardinalhill.org/Louisville/aboutus.html

*Camp KYSOC, Carrollton
Phone 502-732-5333, email cardinalhill.org/camp/index.html

*Cardinal Hill Specialty Hospital, Ft. Thomas
Phone 859-572-3880, email cardinalhill.org/ltach.html

*Cardinal Hill Home Care
Phone 859-367-7148

KENTUCKY AGRABILITY PROGRAM (UK), LEXINGTON
Phone 859-257-1845 (John Hancock), email jhancock@uky.edu

KENTUCKY DEPARTMENT OF FISH AND WILDLIFE,
FRANKFORT
Overcoming Physical Barriers Workshop with Tim Farmer
Phone 800-858-1549, email info.center@ky.gov

KENTUCKY OFFICE OF VOCATIONAL REHABILITATION,
FRANKFORT
Phone 502-564-4440, email ovr.ky.gov/index.htm

SHRINERS HOSPITALS FOR CHILDREN, LEXINGTON
Phone 859-266-2101, email
shrinersshq.org/shc/Lexington/index.html

UNIV. OF LOUISVILLE/KOSAIR CHILDREN'S HOSPITAL,
LOUISVILLE
Phone 502-629-5820, email sully@louisville.edu

The following are special programs associated with Tim's employer, the Kentucky Department of Fish and Wildlife Resources, and can be accessed via the web site (kdfwr.state.ky.us).

ARCHERY IN KENTUCKY'S SCHOOLS
Physical education curriculum involving Olympic-style target archery for 6th-8th grades.

BACKYARD WILDLIFE HABITAT PROGRAM
A program that remedies wildlife habitat loss by engaging schools and suburban homes to create habitat enhancing environments on their own property.

BECOMING AN OUTDOORS WOMAN (BOW)
Workshop that teaches women 18 years or older practical skills regarding the great outdoors.

HABITAT IMPROVEMENT PROGRAM
Department works with private landowners to improve conditions for optimal wildlife environment.

KENTUCKY NETWORK OF OUTDOOR WOMEN (KNOW)
Organization that grew out of BOW workshop. Desire is to expand reach and communication for interested women.

KENTUCKY PRIVATE LANDS COUNCIL
Seeks to coordinate natural resource management help to private landowners.

NATURE PLATE
Program that offers Kentucky vehicle license plates with various nature pictures. Proceeds go to Heritage Land Coservation Fund.

PROJECT WILD
Educational materials emphasizing conservation, environmental and wildlife issues for grades K-12.

RESTORING OUR WILDLIFE HERITAGE
Artists' prints or patches sold for advancement of wildlife education.

SALATO NATIVE PLANT PROGRAM
Education program emphasizing importance of native Kentucky plants to wildlife. Located on grounds of Kentucky Fish and Wildlife Resourses at 1 Game Farm, Frankfort.

STEP OUTSIDE
Web site that encourages shows how one can share their love of the outdoors with friends and relatives.

WILDFLOWER OF THE YEAR
Cooperative effort of the Salato Native Plant Program and the Kentucky Native Plant Society which names a "Wildflower of the Year" from nominations.